The Camondo Museum

Open daily from 10 a.m. to 5 p.m.
except Monday and Tuesday
63, rue de Monceau
75 008 Paris
Tel.: 45 63 26 32

MUSÉES ET MONUMENTS DE FRANCE
COLLECTION DIRECTED BY PIERRE LEMOINE

THE NISSIM DE CAMONDO MUSEUM

NADINE GASC

CHIEF CURATOR OF THE NISSIM DE CAMONDO MUSEUM

GÉRARD MABILLE

CHIEF CURATOR OF THE OBJETS D'ART DEPARTMENT AT THE LOUVRE

FONDATION PARIBAS
UNION CENTRALE DES ARTS DÉCORATIFS
RÉUNION DES MUSÉES NATIONAUX

The collection Musées et
Monuments de France has
been created on the initiative
of the Fondation Paribas

Cover: The Grand Salon
Frontispiece: The Petit Bureau
The walls are covered with cerise
grogram, the original appearance
of which has been restored thanks
to recent treatment.

We are very grateful to Sophie Le Tarnec, who is currently preparing a
dissertation at the Ecole du Louvre on the history and patronage of the
Camondo family, and who kindly put her abundant unpublished
material at our disposal. Her cooperation and that of Nathalie Manuel
have been invaluable.
We also like to thank Gérard Auguier, Christian Baulez, Jean-René
Gaborit, Marie-Noël de Gary, and Tamara Préaud, for their friendly
assistance.
We gratefully remember that it was thanks to the perspicacity and
generosity of Daniel Pasgrimaud, that a clock of the Camondo collection
(Inv. 182), which had fallen prey to vandalism, could be restored.

Foreword

The Camondo Museum, a house built in 1913 and crowded with French eighteenth-century masterpieces, is one man's extraordinary gift to France, his adoptive country, to which he gave everything, including, most importantly, his only son, Nissim, who died for France in aerial combat in 1917.

Over three generations, the Camondo family—lovers, collectors, and patrons of art—applied themselves, with eclecticism, rigour, and passion, to gathering together an exceptional collection of French decorative art.

Moïse de Camondo was a great lover of beauty and perfection, and he has left us a remarkable record of the nineteenth- and early-twentieth-century art of living set in eighteenth-century surroundings.

Now this house belongs to you. It is yours to use as you please: for strolling, observing, learning, admiring, or just feasting your eyes.

With your twentieth-century gaze, you are carrying on the work of Moïse de Camondo, bringing the next in a succession of viewpoints on eighteenth-century art.

Hélène David-Weill
President, Union centrale des arts décoratifs

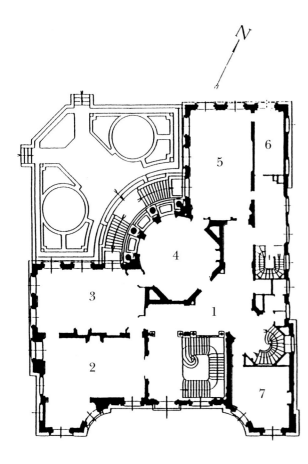

Ground floor

1. Gallery
2. Grand Bureau
3. Grand Salon
4. Salon Huet
5. Dining Room
6. Cabinet des Porcelaines
7. Petit Bureau

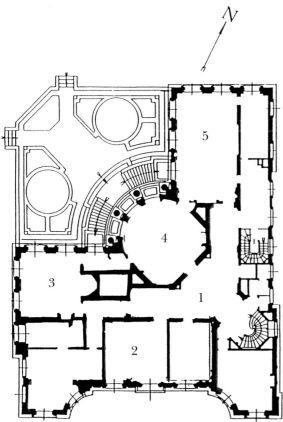

First floor

1. Gallery
2. Nissim's Room
3. Moïse's Room
4. Library
5. Salon Bleu

Note to the reader
The numbers in brackets in the text are those of the 1936 inventory by Jean Messelet
(see Bibliography on page 126).

History of the Museum

A gilt inscription on the pediment of a carriage gateway informs pedestrians on the rue de Monceau that this is the Nissim de Camondo Museum. A marble plaque inside the porch relates the tragic end of the last descendants of this family. All that remains is this museum symbolizing the passion of a collector who had fallen in love with eighteenth-century art: Moïse de Camondo.

He was born in Constantinople in 1860 and spent part of his childhood there, until his father Nissim and his uncle Abraham Behor decided that, in view of the grim economic situation in Turkey, the family had better move to Paris. Beginning in 1860, they came to stay in the capital on several occasions and took turns living there for close to nine years. Thanks to their correspondence, we are kept informed almost from day to day of the problems they faced in completing preparations for their move to Paris. There could be no question of being accepted by French society without conforming to its code of etiquette.

While keeping his brother posted on the political problems of France towards the end of the Second Empire, Abraham Behor shows himself much concerned by a number of material questions: finding a town-house, servants, stables. After some hesitation he settled for a building at number 7 rue de Presbourg which appeared comfortable enough to accommodate the whole family. Nissim moved into a flat with a garden just opposite, at number 6. The family was reunited on 13 October 1869, but Nissim's position obliged him to stay on in Constantinople to welcome Empress Eugénie who was on her way to the inauguration of the Suez canal. Abraham Behor wrote to his brother informing him that everyone was in good health and also—an important detail—that 'Grand-Papa is enjoying himself very much'. Over eighty when he arrived in France, Abraham Salomon was the uncontested patriarch. It was he who had incited his grandsons to open a branch office of their bank 'I. Camondo et Cie' in Paris. Thanks to his energy and his innate business sense, this bank, which he inherited from his brother in 1832, was destined to expand as he made connections with the financial circles of Vienna, London, and Paris.

Abraham Salomon was active in the development of real-estate in Constantinople. He lived in the Galata district with his wife Clara (whom he had married on 25 May 1804), and their son Raphael (1810–1866). As a sign of public recognition, the street on which he lived bore his name and, in order to have easier access to the business district, he built a double helix stairway. The street goes by a different name today, but the stairway still exists.

Respected for the considerable influence he exerted within gov-

The Grand Bureau
The provenance of the oak wainscot (*c.* 1780) is unknown. The Aubusson tapestries depict the *Fables of La Fontaine*, after Jean-Baptiste Oudry.

ernment circles, Abraham Salomon was not insensitive to the distress of the poor. He created support funds and two establishments where the less fortunate could find refuge. He was aware of the fact that poverty was to a certain extent the result of a lack of education and integration, and consequently, in 1854 he decided to open the first Jewish school in that city, paying half of the day-to-day expenses out of his pocket. In his view, the teaching of foreign languages, and particularly of French, was of fundamental importance. Not everybody was of that opinion by any means and, what was worse, his proposal aroused the fanaticism of a certain number of rabbis who strove to have him excommunicated. After considerable tribulations that lead to the school being closed for two years, Abraham Salomon got the better of his opponents—a victory that showed the philanthropist to have been right and proved that this reform in the education of the younger generations had indeed been necessary.

In 1854, as the representative of the Austrian community of Constantinople, he went to Vienna surrounded by his family, to attend the wedding of Emperor Franz Joseph. Although he was Austrian by nationality, his affinities were Italian. It may have been an atavistic fidelity to his distant ancestors who, towards the end of the eighteenth century had settled in Trieste or in the Veneto, then under Austrian domination.

On 18 November 1865 he and all the members of his family obtained the Italian nationality, to the amazement of the inhabitants of the city. Faithful to his ideals and convictions, he moved to Italy, and endowed a Turin orphanage and the city's secondary school with an annual income. He offered his assistance to Victor Emmanuel II who, to thank him, made him a count by decree on 28 April 1867. The title was transmissible through male heirs. As a supreme honour, Abraham Salomon was known thereafter as Count de Camondo. He had a coat of arms and his motto was 'Fides et Caritas'. The gratitude of Victor Emmanuel II also extended to the younger branch of the family and on 15 September 1870, Nissim was also made a count.

Abraham Salomon remained a symbol of total success. A man with a powerful personality, he had accumulated honours and a considerable fortune throughout his lifetime. But the trait that made the man attractive was his unflagging determination to promote education and to assist the destitute. His role in the renovation of Constantinople cannot be denied, for he had within him this need to build, to throw out roots and to serve his faith.

He died in Paris, but his funeral took place in Constantinople on 14 April 1873, with a pomp that was rarely equalled. Life in the city suddenly came to a standstill. The exceptional qualities of their grandfather made a lasting impression on Abraham Behor and Nissim. It was no doubt on his advice that they had bought from Emile Pereire, who owned part of the 'plaine Monceau', a piece of land located at number 61 of the same street. Abraham Behor signed the deed of sale on 28 June 1870 and asked the architect Denis Louis Destors to build a town-house for him. Three days before, Nissim had acquired a town-house located at number 63 and belonging to Monsieur Violet, a public works contractor. He asked the same architect to take care of the interior decoration. Abraham Behor moved into his new home in October 1875.

Coat of arms of the Camondo family

Emile Zola affords us a glimpse of the town-house at number 63 in his book *La Curée*. Conscientious as ever, he took notes on the buildings bordering the Parc Monceau and even went so far as to draw the plans of the new house built by Aristide Rougon, alias Saccard. The distribution of the rooms can be superimposed on that of the Hôtel Violet. The location is the same: 'at the end of the rue de Monceau a short distance from the boulevard Malesherbes ... a large town-house between court and garden'. Same location for the greenhouse too: 'to the right stood a large greenhouse attached to the side of the house and connecting with the ground floor ...', and a bit further on: 'the garden was separated from the parc Monceau by a low fence concealed by a hedge ...' The interior decoration described by Emile Zola is very much like the one conceived by D.L. Destors for the two brothers.

There were frequent receptions in this luxurious setting: high society, the world of the arts and of finance would meet on the occasion of splendid parties that were the talk of Paris. The Camondos kept up the pace of life in Paris. Since it was considered elegant to take the waters, they went to Vichy or Contrexéville, and spent their winters in Nice.

As for his official position, Nissim was appointed president of the Italian committee for the organization of the Universal Exhibition of 1889. He was unable to honour his commitment, however, as he died in January. His brother and his nephew Isaac supervised the completion of this undertaking; the pavilion located on the Champ-de-Mars was a complete success and was praised by all.

At the end of the same year, Abraham Behor also died. At their death, the two brothers left a prosperous bank behind them. They had, since 1872, been associated with the group 'de Paris et des Pays-Bas', and the two institutions would launch a good number of government loans and invest in the construction of several railways, most notably in Spain and in Portugal.

Isaac assumed the direction of the bank, and starting in 1894, as a result of bad health, he was forced to slow down and give up the Constantinople branch. At Isaac's death in 1911, Moïse was no more than an administrator. The bank of 'I. Camondo and Cie' closed down in 1917.

Isaac de Camondo as collector (1851–1911)

Isaac occupied his father's town-house until 1893, before moving to the rue Glück where three apartments were destined to house his collection. In 1874, like his father, he began to take an intense interest in the arts of the Far East. He also began to purchase weapons, and he could occasionally be seen dropping in on Auguste Sichel, an antique dealer of repute and an eminent Japan specialist, or on Samuel Bing. Edmond de Goncourt in his journal, relates a dinner party in the house of Auguste Sichel at which bird's-nest soup was served, in the presence of Camondo, Cernuschi, and others (17 June 1875).

Camondo none the less displayed a certain eclecticism in his tastes. He was drawn to the art of the eighteenth century and purchased several pieces of silverware at the Pichon sale, but it was in 1881, at the Baron Double sale, that he first attracted attention and began assembling his real collection of objects and furniture of this period. The event was without precedent, since all the most important amateurs, gathered together for three days with a view to acquiring the exceptional items they coveted, had raised prices to unprecedented heights.

Isaac was to acquire several prestigious pieces of furniture, some of them having formerly belonged to the royal collections. The furniture of the gilt, carved salon by Foliot, covered with Gobelin and Aubusson tapestries, known as the 'Mobilier des Dieux' (furnishings of the Gods), was knocked down to him at 100,000 F. He bid up to the same amount to acquire *Les Trois Grâces*, a clock attributed to Falconnet. This object remained one of the prides of his collection that he would later complete with certain paintings and drawings by Boucher, Fragonard, Watteau, among others. His passion for the eighteenth century was and is often eclipsed by his love for the painting of his own day, and his name has remained associated with the Impressionist movement. He frequented A. Vollard, Durand-Ruel, A. Bernheim who exhibited works by Cézanne, Corot, Degas, Jongkind, and Monet. Following their advice, he bought a large number of works by these painters, but he also felt affinities for the work of Manet, Pissarro, and Sisley.

Always fascinated by the arts of the Far East, Isaac met another dealer, A. Manzi, who was to play an important role in the development of his collection. It was thanks to him that Isaac assembled nearly 400 Japanese woodcuts, a collection of exceptional value, in which the greatest artists using this technique are represented.

Isaac was much drawn to artistic circles, was constantly in touch with the most prominent scholars, and assisted in the development of new talents. His sensitivity and his scholarship allowed him to contribute to a new trend, a renewal in the realm of music. Having studied composition in his youth, he had written waltzes and polkas for his own enjoyment. He was on friendly terms with Léo Delibes, and they organized a journey to Bayreuth to discover Wagner's music together. Enthused by the Tetralogy, Isaac made a thorough study of this new conception, changed his style and on the 10 March 1904, gave his first concert at the Salle Erard. Encouraged by critical acclaim which acknowledged that he was gifted as a composer, Isaac decided to compose a musical drama, based on an idea by Victor Capoul, the tenor and administrator of the Opéra. Completed in 1906, *The Clown* was performed the 24th, 26th and 29th of April, and the 3rd of May of that year. The performances were given for the benefit of artists and friends of the Opéra of which Isaac was the president and founder. *The Clown* was performed again in 1908 and 1909, first at the Opéra Comique, then at the opera in Marseille and the Vichy Casino.

The surviving elements hardly allow one to form an opinion of its actual artistic merits; only the libretto and the programs of *The Clown* have been preserved in the archives of the Museum—vestiges of a short-lived creation.

Camondo's health declined in the final years. He nevertheless continued to support his friends, including Gabriel Astruc. When the latter brought his plan to build the Théâtre des Champs-Elysées to execution, he always lent him an attentive ear, and was always ready to assist him.

He had never made a secret of his wish to donate his collection to the Louvre and he arranged the conditions of this legacy with meticulous care. His devotion and generosity led to his nomination as president of Les Amis du Louvre and as a member of the commission of the national museums. He would unfortunately not have the pleasure of exercising these functions for long: he died on 7 April 1911 in his apartment at number 82 avenue des Champs-Elysées.

His collection has since been dispersed among several museums, a consequence of their diversity, and it has become difficult to appraise its scope and wealth. But the visitor can, according to his tastes, discover parts of it at the Musée Guimet, the Louvre, the Musée d'Orsay, or the palace of Versailles.

Each one of these groups of works reveal their former owner's sense of quality and rarity and stand among the finest elements of our heritage.

Moïse de Camondo: the Museum (1860–1935)

Upon the death of his mother, in 1910, Moïse inherited the family home at number 63 rue de Monceau. At that time he had already acquired an important part of his collection. Immediately upon his installation in a town-house of the 16th arrondissement, at number 19 rue Hamelin, Moïse developed a passion for eighteenth-century art.

Was this a hereditary trait, or was he under the influence of a fashionable infatuation fuelled by such writers as the Goncourt brothers or by the abundance of objects put up for sale at prestigious auctions such as that of the Baron Double estate? The question is not an easy one to answer. One cannot readily make out the collector's motivations, but it is true none the less, that unlike his cousin Isaac, he remained faithful to the arts of this century. He was somewhat taciturn in temper, and he does not appear to have been particularly drawn to finance. His inclination led him to favour yachting, motor sports, and hunting which he indulged in at Aumont, a property in the vicinity of Senlis that he bought in 1904 and to which he gave the name of his daughter—'Villa Béatrice'.

His marriage with Irène Cahen d'Anvers, celebrated on 14 October 1891, gave him two children: Nissim, born in 1892, and Béatrice, born two years later. He seemed destined to an active social life and an unclouded domestic existence, but the marriage was short-lived and ended in divorce in 1901. Moïse was granted custody of the two children and, as an attentive father, he took their education in hand. He led them on long trips through Europe, and the family was always surrounded by friends when they returned to Aumont for hunting or for riding, which was Beatrice's favourite pastime. When he acquired the Napoleon III town-house at 63 rue de Monceau, Moïse was finally in a position to bring his dream to fulfilment: he had long wanted to have an eighteenth-century building in which to house his collection. With this in view, he called upon the services René Sergent (1865–1927). This last great admirer of the architecture of that period, and in particular of the works of Jacques-Ange Gabriel sought inspiration in the Petit Trianon for the conception of this new residence.

At the end of 1910, the family town-house was demolished. Only the commons remained standing. Sergent submitted his first plans to Moïse. The façade on the main court and the hallway

Count Moïse de Camondo

have many points in common with the domain of which Queen Marie-Antoinette was so fond.

On the garden side these reminiscences are less obvious. With a view to preserving the eighteenth-century spirit, Sergent commissioned the sculptor J. Visseaux to execute a bas-relief that was placed above the rotunda. The terrace leading to the garden was flanked by two stairways whose symmetry contributes to the perfect balance of the building. As for the garden, its arrangement was entrusted to Duchène. The count wishing to be protected from the indiscretion of passers-by, caused an arborescent hedge to be planted. Thanks to a drawing now in the Musée des Arts Décoratifs, we have an exact idea of what Duchène originally proposed: a French garden near the house, an English garden bordering on the park. The plan Sergent had devised for the interior decoration of the house was modified and subjected to various imperatives. For one thing, Moïse had, in the course of the year 1911, purchased most of the antique wainscots that were to be placed in various rooms. First those of the dining room, then of the library which were to determine the height of the windows. And finally, through Lemoine and Leclerc, he acquired the panelling which had been removed from a town-house located at 11 rue Royale in Paris, and which were to decorate the Grand Salon.

The Camondo town-house
Elevation of the garden façade
Drawing by René Sergent
(1865–1927), 1911

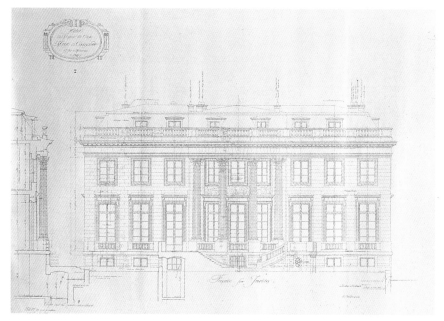

The location of every piece of furniture and of every tapestry was studied with meticulous care. An alcove, for instance, was created in order to provide a worthy setting for the Saunier roll-top desk.

Still, certain items could not be acquired on the market, and it was decided to have copies made. This was the case of the banisters, the main one being executed by the Bagues firm after the original at the Hôtel Dassin in Toulouse. The same principle was followed for a number of espagnolettes, casement bolts and locks, whose reproductions were executed on the basis of various historical documents Moïse already had in his possession.

The count supervised the works and the interior decoration for over three years, in a way that demonstrated both his thoroughness and his commanding wish for this town-house to serve as an appropriate setting for his collection.

The Library
The oak wainscot harmonizes with
the crimson upholstery of the
Louis XVI chairs.

The Grand Salon or Salon Doré
The white and gold wainscot
(*c.* 1775–1780) comes from a private
town-house at 11 rue Royale in Paris.
The seats by Jacob are upholstered
with Aubusson tapestries.

He finally took possession of the building and moved in with his family when the war broke out. And indeed the war was to affect him most profoundly. His son Nissim, a volunteer, was killed in aerial combat in the *département* of Meurthe et Moselle, on 5 September 1917. Overwhelmed with grief, Moïse had to wait until January 1919 to recover the young man's body, so that he might rest in the family vault in Montmartre cemetery. Among the letters of condolence he received, and which have been preserved in the archives of the Museum, there is one that may strike one as particularly touching: 'I cannot know whether my name will mean anything to you. I once dined with you at Madame Cahen's and, more recently, though it also seems extremely remote, you took me to dine with dear Charles Ephrussi of whom I was extremely fond. All these memories appear so distant now.' The letter is signed Marcel Proust!

The death of his son also brought the end of Moïse's line and of his name. If the name of Camondo evokes an undeniable financial success, it is also connected with the promotion of the arts and a patronage which was never interrupted since the times of the grandfather who had taught them everything, and whose perfect disciple Isaac had constantly been. It may have been the will to

Nissim de Camondo (1892–1917)
The Great Staircase
The partly gilt wrought-iron balustrade is a copy by the Bagues firm after that of a private town-house in Toulouse. The statue is attributed to Boizot.

overcome the challenge of time and the cruel strokes of life that determined him to turn this town-house into a museum whose name would continue to stand as the symbol of his passion for the eighteenth century and of his love for his son Nissim. Until the end of his life, he continued to buy and to complete his collection, to perfect its harmony and coherence.

However, Moïse also continued his activities with the national museums. In 1930 he was named vice-president of Les Amis du Louvre, but it was within the framework of the Union Centrale des Arts Décoratifs that he was to play a dominant role. After having presided over the finance commission, he became vice-president

The Salon Bleu, formerly Béatrice de Camondo's room
The colour of the silk with which the walls are covered is called 'the queen's hair'. The wall covering and double curtains 'en gourgouran' were copied after 18th-century originals.

of the U.C.A.D. He provided a generous endowment of 25,000 F in 1920, continued to give financial support to numerous exhibitions and competitions which the Musée des Arts Décoratifs organized, and made a large number of donations. Among other things, he donated a collection of five tie-pins assembled by his father. Surprisingly, and unlike his cousin Isaac, he never mentioned his intention of donating his town-house or his collections. Moïse died on 14 November 1935 and the Museum was inaugurated on 21 December 1936. His dying wish must remain stamped in our memory: 'Desirous of perpetuating the memory of my father, Count Nissim de Camondo and that of my unfortunate son, air force pilot Nissim de Camondo, fallen in aerial combat on the 5th of September 1917, I bequeath to the Musée des Arts Décoratifs my town-house as it stands at the moment of my death. My town-house will bear the name of Nissim de Camondo, my son to whom the house and its collections had been destined.

In bequeathing my town-house and the collections it contains to the State, my purpose is to preserve in its entirety the work to which I have devoted myself, the reconstitution of an artistic dwelling of the eighteenth century. This reconstitution is intended, in my mind, to preserve in France, gathered in particularly appropriate surroundings, the finest examples I have been able to assemble of this decorative art which was one of the glories of France, during the period that I have loved above all others.'

The Salon Huet
The room is called after the famous
series of paintings by Jean-Baptiste
Huet depicting an arcadian
romance. The doors framed by
colonettes were inspired by those of

the Hôtel Jean du Barry at Toulouse.
The white marble mantelpiece
comes from the Hôtel Jean-Joseph
de Laborde, rue Lafitte, Paris.

Furniture

The visitor discovering the Camondo Museum for the first time, may well be most impressed by the furniture. The collection assembled by Count Moïse de Camondo does indeed strike one by its abundance, diversity and homogeneity. More than in any other realm, the collector was able to express here both his sensibility and his ambitions. The collections assembled by Richard Wallace, Henry Clay Frick or Callouste Gulbenkian may contain a larger number of pieces of furniture which are exceptional in their sumptuousness or their provenance, but no collection offers a panorama as subtly and lovingly composed.

In entrusting the construction of his town-house to René Sergent, Moïse de Camondo had deliberately chosen to reconstitute a wealthy aristocratic home of the time of Louis XVI. In doing so he followed his own sensibility, but also that of his age. A setting of such architectural and stylistic coherence obviously imposed similar criteria on the choice of furniture. With the exception of a few seats and above all of two extraordinary lacquer corner cupboards, the furniture belongs either to the final phase of Louis XV style, generally referred to as transitional style, or to the Louis XVI period.

Even though, on the whole, rocaille ornamentation is rather poorly represented in the collection, there is the outstanding exception of two *encoignures* (corner cupboards) in black and gold lacquer, rightly attributed to the famous BVRB [36]. The significance of these initials remained a mystery for a long time. Only in 1957 did the scholarly research of J.P. Baroli reveal that this enigmatic stamp referred to the name of three *ébénistes* (cabinet-makers) of Dutch extraction, the Van Risen Burghs, who succeeded one another from father to son, each one of them named Bernard. The personality of Bernard II was surely the most remarkable. Born about 1696, he got his mastership before 1730. His entire career was spent at the service of the great *marchands merciers*—Hébert, Duvaux, Poirier—whose shops presented the most elegant clientele of Paris with all that was most rare and precious in matters of curios, textiles, and *ébénisterie* furniture. The decisive role played by these shops in the evolution of taste and in the constant renewal of creation has often been stressed. They favoured the use of new materials, lacquer or porcelain, which the artisans, who generally have remained anonymous, knew how to use to the best effect.

It may have been in view of concealing the place of origin of these masterpieces that some of the *ébénistes'* stamps were intentionally made undecipherable. This was the case of the BVRB, which Bernard Van Risen Burgh was already using in 1735. He retired in

The Count's Room
Mathieu-Guillaume Cramer
(?–1794), master in Paris in 1771
Chest of drawers, *c.* 1775
Oak, rosewood, amarant, boxwood, chased and gilt bronze, blue marble
0.900 x 1.420 x 0.620. Inv. 636
Georges Jacob (1739–1814), master in Paris in 1765
Armchair 'à la reine', *c.* 1780
Walnut, carved and painted
0.910 x 0.620 x 0.520. Inv. 647

1764, after having sold his stock to his son, and died in 1767.

In terms of its technical and aesthetic qualities, his production rates among the most representative of the rocaille manner; it allies a perfect execution of geometric or floral marquetry, gilt bronzes, porcelain plaques or lacquer panels, the increased use of the latter being a particular consequence of the *ébéniste*'s creative talent.

It is now known that Van Risen Burgh, an occasional purveyor to the Royal *Garde-Meuble* (Royal Household) by the intermediary of Hébert the furniture dealer, had already executed, in 1737, for Queen Marie Leszczynska's apartments at Fontainebleau, a chest of drawers decorated with Japanese lacquer, which can be seen in the Louvre today. We have every reason to believe that this is the oldest known piece of furniture illustrating a technique which was often used by BVRB in subsequent years.

The *encoignures* (corner cupboards) of the Camondo Museum, acquired in 1911, are a splendid example of this. The doors of

Pierre Hache (1703–1776), master in Grenoble
Etagère of a corner cupboard, *c.* 1770
Walnut, boxwood, ebony, fruitwood
0.820 x 0.230. Inv. 654

Attributed to Bernard Van Risen Burgh (*c.* 1696–1765), master in Paris before 1735
Encoignure (corner cupboard), *c.* 1750
Oak, Japanese lacquer, European lacquer, chased and gilt bronze, red and brown marble
0.920 x 0.720 x 0.930. Inv. 36

these cupboards are decorated with Japanese black and gold lacquer which was probably borrowed from a folding screen or a chest. The rest of it, in *vernis Martin*, displays the skill with which Parisian workshops managed to imitate oriental models. The bronzes, in a noble and majestic rococo style, are beautifully chased and gilt. In their ample proportions, these two pieces clearly demonstrate that the talent of BVRB could go beyond gracefulness and elegance, and achieve a powerful monumentality.

Pierre Garnier, born in 1720, obtained his mastership in 1742. His career was a long one, since he lived until 1800. His first works are still in rococo style, but already in the 1760s, he showed the

influence of the engravings of Delafosse, Lorrain, and Neufforge, and was among the first to try his hand at neo-classicism, an innovation he was strongly encouraged to pursue by some of his clients, such as the Marquis de Marigny, brother of Madame de Pompadour and director of the King's Buildings. Garnier also created furniture for the Duchess de Mazarin and for Marshal de Contades at the castle of Montgeoffroy.

The two pieces of furniture of the Salon Huet [189] were acquired separately by Moïse de Camondo who bought them from Seligmann, the first in 1898, the other in 1928. They are particularly characteristic of the innovations ventured by this craftsman. The sinuous design of the front and legs which are still Louis XV belong to the final stage of rococo, whereas the ormolu corner mounts and the perfectly rectilinear framing of the Japanese

Pierre Garnier (*c.* 1720–1800), master in Paris in 1742
Commode à vantaux, *c.* 1770
Oak, amarant, snakewood, boxwood, ebony, Japanese lacquer, aventurine lacquer, chased and gilt bronze, 'brèche violette' marble
0.860 x 1.590 x 0.480. Inv. 189

Jean-François Oeben (1721–1763),
master in Paris in 1761
Bureau à cylindre (roll-top desk),
c. 1760
Oak, rosewood, sycamore, boxwood,
pearwood, lemonwood, amarant,
ebony, ash burr, chased and gilt
bronze
0.980 x 0.820 x 0.520. Inv. 191

On page 27:
Detail of the above illustration

lacquer panels bordered with aventurine lacquer are unambiguous signs of the rise of classicism, then referred to as the 'Greek' style. It will be noted that the drawers of the *commode à vantaux*, with their corner shelves, are concealed behind two doors—a trait quite typical of the evolution of forms and structures in the last third of the eighteenth century.

Jean-François Oeben was the exact contemporary of Garnier. Born in 1721 in the vicinity of Aachen, he must have moved to Paris about 1740 or 1745, where he may have completed his apprenticeship. Between 1751 and 1754, he was employed in Boulle's workshop in the Louvre, and when it closed down, Oeben was given the use of a new workshop at the Gobelins, where he remained until 1761. At the same time he was given the title of 'ébéniste du roi'.

In 1756, he moved to another space at the Arsenal, where he once more enjoyed the royal protection. Oeben was soon to make this his permanent workshop, and remained there until his death in 1763. The inventory of his estate offers some information on his customers, which included Madame de Pompadour, who made him one of her chief suppliers, the Duke d'Aumont, the Duchess de Lauragais, the Duchess de Brancas, Grimod de la Reynière, Choiseul, and Argenson.

Oeben's reputation rested both on the perfection and beauty of his floral marquetry and on ingenious and practical mechanisms with which he improved his works. These are indeed the qualities that are apparent in the little *bureau à cylindre* (roll-top desk) now in the Salon Huet [191].

It is rightly presumed that this type of furniture was invented by Oeben himself about 1760. The high point of his achievement, the Louis XV desk of Versailles, delivered by Riesener in 1769, had been begun much earlier by Oeben, since the 1763 inventory reveals that the unfinished desk was then in the Arsenal workshop. The desk at the Camondo Museum might be its small-scale prefiguration. It has been compared to an article rather similar in shape and size, described in 1763 and entrusted to Oeben by Madame de Pompadour in order that it should 'be mended and repaired': 'one rosewood desk, 33 inches long [89.3 cm] by 18 inches deep [48.6 cm], 3 feet high [97.5 cm] including the baluster, the front sliding out on grooves and the top closing with a roller, on the lower part of this desk is a shelf between the legs ...' With the exception of this last point which excludes any attempt to prove that in either case we are dealing with the same item, it does appear that Madame de Pompadour's desk was very similar to the one that Moïse de Camondo bought from Seligmann in 1899 and which had belonged to the famous and high-living Boni de Castellane. As often happens in Oeben's production, the silhouette of this item, with its delicate proportions, is still strongly influenced by the animated Louis XV forms. Admirable is the dazzling virtuosity of the marquetry in which the floral compositions assemble the most varied sorts of wood.

Roger Vandercruse, known as Lacroix or again, as RVLC, as in one of his stamps, was the son of a large family of Flemish origin. Born in 1728, he obtained his mastership in Paris in 1755 and died in 1799. The marriages of his sisters established a link between him and several of his colleagues; Marie-Marguerite married Simon

Oeben, while Françoise-Marguerite was to marry, first Jean-François Oeben, then Jean-Henri Riesener. If we add that Marie-Catherine Oeben, sister of the two *ébénistes* married Martin Carlin and then, after having become a widow, Gaspard Schneider, we will get some idea of the closeness of family ties which spontaneously formed in the Parisian circle of furniture makers of the eighteenth century.

Roger Vandercruse worked for Migeon, the merchant and *ébéniste*, for the *marchand mercier* Poirier, and he also worked with Jean-François Oeben. Joubert caused him to be occasionally employed at the Royal *Garde-Meuble*. His production is abundantly represented at the Camondo Museum, where eight pieces of furniture bear his stamp.

Two small tables *en chiffonnière* in transitional style—a round one [62], made of violet and rosewood, decorated with crosscut floral marquetry, and an oval one of green stained wood, decorated with foliage and shaded points [131]—belong to a type of light furniture which was abundantly turned out by this *ébéniste*.

It is no doubt the collaboration between RVLC and Poirier, the

Roger Vandercruse (Lacroix) (1728–1799), master in Paris in 1755
Secrétaire 'à la Bourgogne', *c.* 1760
Oak, walnut, snakewood, amarant, rosewood, boxwood, ebony, chased and gilt bronze
0.720 x 0.650 x 0.460. Inv. 345

Table 'en cabaret', *c.* 1760
Oak, limewood, varnish, plaque of soft-paste Sèvres porcelain, chased and gilt bronze
0.690 x 0.330 x 0.270. Inv. 194

marchand mercier that produced the famous *table en cabaret* [194], coated with *vernis Martin* and completed with a Sèvres soft-paste porcelain top. Its general shape closely reminds one of a whole group of identical tables turned out by BVRB from 1758, and apparently based on a conception of Poirier's, who regularly entrusted his *ébénistes* with elements purchased from Sèvres. The originally white varnished decoration of the table in the Camondo Museum has discoloured with time, hence the present yellow hue which no longer harmonizes with the colours of the porcelain. Bought in 1934 from Bensimon, it may have been one of the count's very last acquisitions.

Roger Vandercruse (Lacroix) (1728–1799), master in Paris in 1755
Round table 'en chiffonnière', *c.* 1760
Oak, walnut, rosewood, violet wood, boxwood, chased and gilt bronze.
0.750 x 0.370. Inv. 62

Oval table 'en chiffonnière', *c.* 1775
Oak, violet wood, rosewood, San Domingo lemonwood, sycamore, ebony, boxwood, chased and gilt bronze
0.740 x 0.480 x 0.360. Inv. 131

The family and professional ties that had been established between Lacroix and Oeben no doubt account for the technical and aesthetic characteristics of the *secrétaire à la Bourgogne* that can be seen in the Petit Bureau [345]. This type of furniture does indeed seem to be a creation of Jean-François Oeben. An ingenious mechanism causes a tier of drawers to emerge, which, when the desk is closed, completely disappears beneath the tabletop. The cube motif of the marquetry is equally characteristic of the works

Claude-Charles Saunier (1735–1807), master in Paris in 1752
Bureau à cylindre (roll-top desk), c. 1780
Oak, flamed mahogany, chased and gilt bronze, white veined marble
1.230 x 1.330 x 0.680. Inv. 55

Claude-Charles Saunier (1735–1807), master in Paris in 1752
Table 'en cabaret', c. 1770
Oak, pine, rosewood, amarant, sycamore, boxwood, chased and gilt bronze, 'brèche d' Alep' marble
0.700 x 0.430 x 0.330. Inv. 348

Roger Vandercruse (Lacroix) (1728–1799), master in Paris in 1755
Chest of drawers, c. 1770
Oak, rosewood, sycamore, amarant, boxwood, chased and gilt bronze, brocatelle marble
0.890 x 1.300 x 0.590. Inv. 339

of the king's *ébéniste* who exercised a strong influence on his brother-in-law. The latter was responsible for a fine chest of drawers in transitional style, which also bears Leleu's stamp (no doubt as a result of a restoration undertaken by Leleu) [339].

Claude-Charles Saunier (1735–1807), who became a master in 1752, belonged to the same generation as RVLC. His work is usually characterized by sobriety, elegance, and a thoroughly classical austerity. The base of his *table en cabaret* in the Petit Bureau with its hollowed-out marble top [348], still shows the Louis XV silhouette in its legs.

The three pieces now in the Grand Bureau, on the other hand—

a roll-top desk [55], a fall-front desk [54], and a low bookcase [52], all three of them soberly veneered in mahogany and enhanced with gilt bronze mounts—are entirely in the Louis XVI style of the 1780s.

Upon Oeben's death in 1763 the smoldering rivalry between his two best apprentices, Riesener and Leleu, erupted in public. One should not be tempted to underestimate Leleu's talent simply by the fact that he did not emerge as the winner.

Born in 1729, he obtained his mastership in 1764 but, having been evicted by his rival, he was unable to succeed his master at

Jean-François Leleu (1729–1807),
master in Paris in 1764
Secrétaire à abattant (fall-front
desk), *c.* 1775
Oak, amarant, sycamore, ebony,
boxwood, violet wood, rosewood,
holly, chased and gilt bronze, white
veined marble
1.060 x 1.430 x 0.440. Inv. 584

Candelabra
End of the 18th century
Chased and gilt bronze
1.040 x 0.420. Inv. 247
Jean-François Leleu (1729–1807),
master in Paris in 1761
Bas armoire, *c.* 1780
Oak, rosewood, sycamore, boxwood,
holly, yoke-elm, pearwood, amarant,
ebony, chased and gilt bronze,
Sarancolin marble
1.010 x 0.890 x 0.440. Inv. 237

the head of the Arsenal workshop. He none the less acquired a prestigious clientele, including the Prince de Condé, the Marquess de Laborde and the Duke d'Uzès. His highly personal style is marked by a penchant for monumental, sometimes austere forms, usually covered with handsomely executed marquetry. Such are indeed the characteristics of the *bas armoires* in the Grand Bureau [49] and in the dining room [237], whose floral marquetry clearly reflects Oeben's influence.

One may observe the daring with which Leleu conceived furniture without legs, resting directly on the ground in the manner of an architectural base. As for the fall-front desk in the Library [584], its very fine silhouette and its patterns of marquetry in the shape of lozenges and rosettes invite a comparison with a large *bas armoire* now at the Château de Ménars, and with a desk belonging to the Getty Museum.

More than any other, Jean-Henri Riesener embodied the perfection of Parisian cabinet-making under Louis XVI. Like many of his colleagues, he was born outside France, in Westphalia, in 1734. He settled in Paris, probably about 1754, completing his apprenticeship with Oeben at the Arsenal, the workshop which he was to take over at his master's death in 1763. In 1767, as though to set a

seal on this inheritance, Riesener married Oeben's widow, née Vandercruse, and finally gained the rank of master in 1768. In 1774, Joubert went into retirement and conceded his functions of 'ébéniste du roi' to Riesener by contract. This ensured Riesener a privileged situation, since he became the sole *ébéniste*-purveyor of the Royal Household. Thenceforth, and for a period of ten years, he ran the most productive workshop in town and had an exceptionally brilliant career. It has been established that he provided the Crown with more than 700 items of furniture between 1774 and 1784—besides which he also supplied a large number of other clients.

But Riesener's name is above all associated with countless commissions received from Queen Marie-Antoinette, for whom he conceived his most outstanding masterpieces. One rarely finds this degree of harmony between the talent of a creator of genius and a patron whose tastes are subject to no restrictions.

Working in turn for Versailles, Trianon, Marly, Fontainebleau, Compiègne, the Tuileries, or Saint-Cloud, the *ébéniste* turned out countless pieces of furniture that are among the most luxurious and refined, with floral or geometric marquetry, sometimes with plain unadorned veneer, always enhanced with finely chased gilt bronze mounts in which classical motifs and naturalistically rendered flowers are assembled with a superb sense of balance.

This remarkably active productivity was brutally cut off in 1784, when Thiérry de Ville-d'Avray was appointed head of the Royal Household. Wishing to be noted for his zeal and good management, he settled on a policy of economy. Of all the new dispositions he enforced, the most unjustified was the eviction of Riesener, whom he accused of inflating his bills. Consequently, the activity at the workshop significantly decreased, although the queen, by way of her personal *garde-meuble*, kept him in favour until the dark years of the Revolution. Meanwhile, Riesener went on working for his private clients, but the fall of the Ancien Régime was none the less fatal to him. Old, ruined, and forgotten, he died in obscurity in 1806.

Camondo bought the cabinet [120] now in the Grand Salon from Wildenstein in 1909. Nothing is known as yet of its provenance, but it is no doubt a splendid specimen of the countless commissions Riesener received from his private clients. The general shape is that of a chest of drawers, but its highly original conception makes it very different in fact: the front has neither drawers nor hinged doors, but is divided into two curtains of slats that slide to either side. The numerous drawers inside suggest that it was designed for a very specific purpose, such as a collection of curios or medallions.

This cabinet is quite easily situated in the evolution of Riesener's craft. Certain motifs in bronze, such as the legs and the apron had already been used by the *ébéniste* for a chest of drawers conceived in 1774 for Louis XVI's chamber in Versailles (Windsor). The large panel of floral marquetry decorating the central part is still in a manner inherited from Oeben. On the other hand, the predominance of straight lines, the very classical bronze corners and frieze, the lozenge-shape marquetry of the lateral compartments clearly belong to the more personal style that Riesener developed about 1780. It should be noted that this piece has

Claude-Charles Saunier
(1735–1807), master in Paris in 1752
Secrétaire à abattant (fall-front desk), *c.* 1780
Oak, mahogany, chased and gilt bronze, white veined marble
1.420 x 1.330 x 0.450. Inv. 54

Jean Henri Riesener (1734–1806), master in Paris in 1768
Cabinet with sliding curtains, *c.* 1775–1780
Oak, amarant, sycamore, ash burr, snakewood, boxwood, ebony, chased and gilt bronze, 'brèche violette' marble
0.940 x 1.370 x 0.600. Inv. 120

The Vestibule
Jean-Henri Riesener (1734–1806),
master in Paris in 1768
Bureau plat (flat-topped desk),
c. 1780
Oak, flamed mahogany, chased and
gilt bronze
0.780 x 1.720 x 0.940. Inv. 4

Long-case clock, *c.* 1780
Works by Lepaute, Royal Clock-
maker (1727–1802)
Oak, mahogany, chased and
gilt bronze
3.000 x 0.850 x 0.430. Inv. 24

many points in common with two chests of drawers completed by Riesener in 1780 for the queen's apartments in Compiègne.

Mahogany veneered furniture enhanced with relatively sober gilt bronze mounts is frequently found in Riesener's production starting in the 1780s. Two items of furniture in the Museum's collections belong to this category: the large *bureau plat* (flat-topped desk) in the vestibule, bought from Fabre in 1925 [4], and the upright *secrétaire* in Nissim's room on the first floor [754].

One little table [347] presented in the Petit Bureau is particularly affecting because of the memories attached to it: it is a precious trace of the last work undertaken by Riesener for Marie-

Martin Carlin (*c.* 1730–1785), master in Paris in 1766
Bonheur-du-jour, *c.* 1766–1770
Oak, rosewood, sycamore, amarant, ebony, plaques of Sèvres soft-paste porcelain (1766), chased and gilt bronze
0.810 x 0.670 x 0.420. Inv. 126

Jean-Henri Riesener (1734–1806), master in Paris in 1768
Trough-shaped table 'en chiffonnière', delivered in 1788 for the 'cabinet intérieur' of Queen Marie-Antoinette at Saint-Cloud
Oak, rosewood, sycamore, amarant, pearwood, boxwood, chased and gilt bronze
0.780 x 0.770 x 0.350. Inv. 347

Antoinette. Delivered on 1 September 1788 for the queen's 'cabinet intérieur' at Saint-Cloud, its description is found in the inventory made in 1789. It was no doubt still there during the last summer the royal family spent at Saint-Cloud in 1790. Such a piece of furniture had a wide variety of uses: the high edge around the top (which gives it the trough-shape), makes it into a sewing table; but a side drawer with a leather lid and a silver-plated metal pen-holder also makes it a writing table.

Pierre Verlet has rightly observed that the marquetry of lozenges and dots matches that of the lacquered writing table completed for the same room by Weisweiler in 1784 (Musée du Louvre).

While Riesener pursued his brilliant career under royal protection, the *ébénistes* of the Faubourg Saint-Antoine displayed an equally productive initiative, quite often in collaboration with the *marchands merciers.* Such was the case of Martin Carlin (1730–1785), also German by birth, who became master in Paris in 1766. He married Jean-François Oeben's sister in 1759, and appears to have worked with Oeben himself. Simon Poirier, *marchand mercier,* soon made use of his talent and, between 1766 and 1778, called upon him to produce small pieces of furniture decorated with plates of porcelain, bought from the Manufacture de Sèvres. Later on, together with the *marchand mercier* Darnault, Carlin began producing lacquered furniture, particularly for the Château de Bellevue; a small table in the Camondo Museum [58], veneered with mahogany, bears the mark of that château along with the *ébéniste*'s stamp and might be connected with these commissions.

One of Carlin's most attractive creations is his series of *bonheurs-du-jour* which included the one Moïse de Camondo bought from Seligmann in 1899 [126]. Eleven similar pieces of furniture in all have been identified so far: besides the one in the Camondo Museum, we may mention those found in Waddesdon Manor, in the collection of the Duke of Buccleuch in Boughton, in the Bowes Museum, two in the Metropolitan Museum, and two in the Huntington Collection in San Marino, California. They all have the same aspect of a small *bureau à gradin* resting on cabriole legs; the cabinet-work proper, rosewood veneer on the legs and frames, marquetry on the back, is eclipsed by the number of Sèvres soft-paste porcelain plates; there are seventeen in all, decorated with polychrome floral motifs and green and gold borders. A large drawer in the frieze serves as a writing surface. A similar piece of furniture was delivered by Poirier to Madame du Barry in 1768; the Countess d'Artois also owned one. The marks on the porcelain plates of the different pieces allow us to date them between 1765 and 1774, and to place the date of conception of this type of *bonheur-du-jour* around 1765, which is confirmed by the manifest transitional style of these items.

A recent study of the plates on the furniture of the Camondo collection has revealed that several of them are signed by the flower painter Catrice. Since nine of them bear the mark of the year 1766 and none of a later date, it may be supposed that the item in the Camondo Museum is one of the earliest of this series. It was also the collaboration between Carlin and Poirier that led to the creation of a model that was abundantly produced by the *ébéniste*: the round tables, both trough-shaped and *'en chiffonnière'* resting on three cabriole legs, covered with rosewood or ebony veneer and adorned with plates of soft-paste porcelain from Sèvres. At least thirteen items of this type of sewing table have been identified. The one in the Camondo Museum [133] was bought from Lion in 1913.

The career of Adam Weisweiler has some points in common with that of Carlin. He was born in the Rhineland in 1744, and by the time he got married in 1777 he was already a Parisian. He became master in 1778, and settled in the Faubourg Saint-Antoine.

Practically all his activity was connected with the circle of the *marchands merciers*: Daguerre, who succeeded Poirier in 1778,

Martin Carlin (*c.* 1730–1785), master in Paris in 1766
Round table 'en cabaret', *c.* 1775
Oak, rosewood, sycamore, boxwood, ebony, plaques of Sèvres soft-paste porcelain, chased and gilt bronze
0.730 x 0.410. Inv. 133

Adam Weisweiler (1744–1820),
master in Paris in 1778
Serving table, *c.* 1785
Oak, ebony, pewter, gilt and
patinated bronze, green 'antique'
marble
0.830 x 0.570 x 0.410. Inv. 242

Console dessert, *c.* 1780
Oak, mahogany, chased and gilt
bronze, white veined marble, mirror
1.000 x 1.900 x 0.550. Inv. 238

employed him constantly. As a result of this he became the supplier of the French court, of the Queen of Naples, of Maria Feodorovna, daughter-in-law of Catherine II, and of the cream of French and English aristocracy. The Revolution in no way hampered his career, and he was still active under the Empire, apparently until 1809. He died in 1820.

Aside from some background effects now and then, Weisweiler rarely used marquetry of the traditional kind; instead he preferred plain veneer, in mahogany or ebony, as can be seen on the two porphyry-topped consoles of the Grand Salon [122]. But his style is best revealed in his use of precious materials: Japanese lacquer, porcelain plaques, and pietradura marquetry. Some of his works, in which gilt bronze plays a greater role than wood, show a surprising audacity.

The Camondo dining room contains a remarkable selection of his works. There is a large mahogany console [238] backed with mirrors, with legs in the shape of small tapering pillars and two white marble shelfs connecting the legs; the gilt bronze frieze on the entablature shows a motif often favoured by this *ébéniste.*

Two very elegant little tables [242] in the same room were acquired in 1931 in Berlin at the Stroganoff sale; they are veneered with ebony and have a white-speckled, green marble top, four tapering fluted legs and a cross-stretcher bearing a bronze jug, which allows us to establish a connection with a similar piece of furniture described in 1796 in the inventory of the estate of Dominique Daguerre, *marchand mercier.*

Weisweiler widely used Japanese lacquered panels, often borrowed from dismantled chests or screens. A splendid example of this can be found in the two *bas armoires* of the Grand Salon which were bought from Seligmann in 1921 [121]. The black and gold harmony of the lacquer panels decorated with flowered vases is supplemented on the sides, by European varnishes. The highly architectural composition of the whole is energetically stressed by fluted pilasters and addorned with a sumptuous ornamentation of gilt bronze.

David Roentgen holds a special place among Parisian cabinetmakers, in that his career unfolded chiefly in Germany. Born in Neuwied in the Rhineland in 1743, he took over his father's workshop in 1772. He made several stays in Paris, first in 1774 and then in 1779, after which he came to the attention of the royal family from whom he obtained commissions. In 1780, having been obliged to solicit his reception as *maître ébéniste* in Paris, he opened a shop there, but this did not prevent him from keeping his workshop in Neuwied until 1795.

His production is notable for the perfection of his marquetry and for the inventiveness of his mechanisms and constructions. Moïse de Camondo bought a little oval table from Seligmann in 1901 [130], which now stands in the Grand Salon and is highly characteristic of Roentgen's production. A *bas armoire*, displayed in the first-floor gallery [305], bears the stamp DAVID, a signature he adopted after his reception as master in 1780.

Also of Rhenish origin, Mathieu Cramer, was received as master in Paris in 1771 and declared himself bankrupt in 1790. In the course of these twenty years he produced a large quantity of furniture in the transitional style and then in that of Louis XVI,

Adam Weisweiler (1744–1820),
master in Paris in 1778
Bas armoire, *c.* 1780
Japanese lacquer, ebony, aventurine
lacquer, chased and gilt bronze,
brocatelle marble
1.000 x 0.860 x 0.420. Inv. 121

Commode, *c.* 1785
Oak, flamed mahogany, imitation
Wedgwood biscuit plaque, chased
and gilt bronze, 'fleur de pêcher'
marble, mirror
0.980 x 1.340 x 0.520. Inv. 123

making considerable use of geometrical marquetry and background effects. The fine chest of drawers in transitional style epitomizes his production [636]. Moïse de Camondo had it placed in his own room after having bought it from Seligmann in 1892.

The large number of works by Charles Topino appearing in the Camondo collection is significant of the success this *ébéniste* enjoyed among collectors of ancient furniture at the outset of the twentieth century.

Topino, a native of Arras, became a master in 1773. He seems to have been too carefree and went bankrupt sixteen years later, in 1789. He has left us a number of charming little pieces of furni-

Charles Topino, master in Paris
in 1773
Table 'en chiffonnière' (chiffonier),
c. 1775
Oak, rosewood, amarant, boxwood,
sycamore, chased and gilt bronze,
'brèche d'Alep' marble
0.740 x 0.540 x 0.370. Inv. 60

David Roentgen (1741–1809),
master in Paris in 1780
Oval table, *c.* 1780
Oak, rosewood, sycamore, boxwood,
ebony, chased and gilt bronze
0.730 x 0.730 x 0.500. Inv. 130

ture, such as *tables en chiffonnière* [60, 349], *bonheurs-du-jour* [639], consoles [637], or imaginative dressing tables [755bis].

Although cabinets and seats were produced in the eighteenth century by craftsmen belonging to a single corporation, that of the *menuisiers-ébénistes*, a real distinction did exist between these two groups. While the *ébénistes* (cabinet-makers), using the techniques of veneering and marquetry, had settled around the Faubourg Saint-Antoine, the *menuisiers* (joiners), who worked only in solid wood, with carvings, carved mouldings, painted or gilt, were to be found rue de Cléry, in the parish of Notre-Dame de Bonne-Nouvelle. There they built and assembled the consoles, seats, screens, and folding screens which were then entrusted to the sculptors, gilders and finally to the upholsterers.

Count de Camondo assembled a splendid collection of *menuiserie* furniture which perfectly matches the *ébénisterie* furniture described above. Although Louis XV furniture is not as lavishly represented as Louis XVI, the collection does include two sets of works which significantly illustrate the 'dialogue' between Parisian and provincial *menuisiers*.

Nicolas-Quinibert Foliot (1706–1776), master in 1729, was the maker of the eight *chaises à la Reine* [69], now on display in the Grand Bureau. They are upholstered with Aubusson tapestry but unfortunately no longer have their original coat of paint. Apart from being purveyor to the Royal Household, Foliot also worked for private custom, as attested by this sober and elegant set.

Pierre Nogaret was born in Paris in 1720; by 1744 he was in Lyons, where he became master in 1745. Until his death in 1771, he turned out a large number of chairs, many of which are in carved and waxed walnut with cane seats and backs; their somewhat accentuated curves lend a highly personal quality to his production. A series of grey-painted, cane armchairs in the first-floor gallery was produced in his workshop [462].

Several of the seats now in the Camondo Museum belong to the transitional style of the years 1765–1775. The first one deserving of mention is the large carved and gilt beech *canapé à joues* [64], in the Grand Bureau. With its ample forms—still Louis XV—and its remarkable carved ornamentation of classical inspiration, it is somewhat reminiscent of the work of Foliot or Delanois. Unfortunately, it lacks any mark that might establish its origin.

Jean-René Nadal (Nadal l'Aîné), master in 1756, was especially

Charles Topino, master in Paris in 1773
Heart-shaped dressing table, *c.* 1770
Oak, rosewood, amarant, boxwood, yoke-elm, violet wood, chased and gilt bronze
0.750 x 0.480 x 0.470. Inv. 755bis

Joseph Feuerstein (1733–1809), master in Paris in 1767
Encoignure (corner cupboard), *c.* 1775
Oak, white and blue lacquer, oval camaïeu medallion representing *Venus and Cupid*, chased and gilt bronze, white veined marble
0.880 x 0.470 x 0.340. Inv. 124

noted for his seating furniture in transitional style. Yet the surprising desk armchair [136] in the Grand Salon shows practically no trace of the Louis XV style. Acquired at the Jacques Doucet sale in 1912, it bears the mark CDT, recently identified as being that of the *garde-meuble* of Count d'Artois; it was part of a set which has been dispersed, and which was delivered in 1775 for the prince's 'cabinet intérieur' in Versailles, on the second floor of the south wing. The prototype may well have been created by Gondoin.

Georges Jacob was undoubtedly the most famous Parisian *menuisier* of the Louis XVI period; he was also the most inventive and original. He was born in Burgundy in 1739 and came to Paris at

Pierre Nogaret (1720–1771),
master in Lyons
Armchair 'à la reine', *c.* 1750
Walnut, carved and painted, cane;
movable cushion covered in 'petit point' tapestry
0.950 x 0.660 x 0.530. Inv. 462

Nicolas-Quinibert Foliot (1706–1776)
Chair 'à la reine', *c.* 1755
Beech, carved; upholstered in
Aubusson tapestry representing
The Fables of La Fontaine
0.950 x 0.570 x 0.530. Inv. 69

Canapé à joues, *c.* 1770–1775
Beech, carved and gilt
1.150 x 2.000 x 0.850. Inv. 64

about the age of sixteen, working for a while as a journeyman in Louis Delanois' workshop, before becoming a master in 1765. He settled first rue de Cléry, then rue Meslay. In 1773 he received his first commissions for the Royal Household.

Although he was never a supplier in title, this did not prevent him from contributing to the furnishing of Versailles, Trianon, Fontainebleau, Compiègne, and Saint-Cloud. The queen, the counts of Provence and Artois, the royal princes and the high nobility frequently called upon his talent, for he excelled in creating new models, that were original in both shape and decoration. He was

Georges Jacob (1739–1814), master
in Paris in 1765
Foot-stool, *c.* 1780
Beech, walnut, carved and gilt
0.310 x 0.620 x 0.380. Inv. 201

Claude Chevigny, master in Paris
in 1768
Bergère (easy chair), *c.* 1780
Walnut, carved and gilt
1.020 x 0.730 x 0.740. Inv. 66

Jean-René Nadal l'Aîne (1733–?),
master in Paris in 1756
Desk armchair, delivered in 1775
for the 'cabinet intérieur' of Count
d'Artois at Versailles
Beech, carved and gilt; upholstered
in leather
0.980 x 0.660 x 0.500. Inv. 136

also among the first to produce solid mahogany chairs, following a fashion originated in England. Jacob survived the Revolution with ease thanks to his connections with David. He made the shop over to his sons in 1796, but returned to work after the death of the elder son in 1803, and assisted the younger one, François-Honoré, until 1812. He died in 1814.

There are many works by Jacob at the Camondo Museum: in the Grand Salon, for instance, is a set of carved and gilt wooden chairs [135], upholstered with Aubusson tapestry, formerly in the Richard Wallace collection; in the Salon Huet is a foot-stool [201]; and finally, the count's room contains two remarkably carved armchairs *à la Reine* [647].

While Jacob, who worked entirely independently, dominated the realm of Parisian *menuisiers*, Boulard and Sené, who were both attached to the Royal *Garde-Meuble*, had rather more laborious careers, it would seem. Their production, while less individualistic, is nevertheless of high quality.

Jean-Baptiste Boulard (1725–1789), *maître menuisier* (master cabinet-maker) in 1754, worked for the Royal Household from 1777 onwards. In this capacity he executed a large number of pieces of furniture for the royal apartments in Versailles, Fontainebleau, and Compiègne. It was in December 1784 that Louis XVI decided to renew the furnishing of the Salon des Jeux, his game room in Versailles; the four *encoignures* provided by Riesener in 1775 were kept, but otherwise the furniture was entirely renewed.

Executed under the responsibility of the sculptor Hauré, the new items including thirty-six chairs, a screen, and a carved and gilt folding screen, upholstered in crimson and gold brocade, were delivered in 1785. The chairs, by Boulard, were carved by Vallois and Vassal; the Versailles Museum has recovered nineteen of them, two others are in Chantilly. The screen has not yet been found; the four-leafed folding screen, however, is the one Moïse de Camondo placed in the Salon Huet [202]. Pierre Verlet, and Christian Baulez after him, have managed to reconstruct its history: the wax model was made by Martin; the carving was entrusted to Leroux with motifs of laurel and ears of wheat identical with those on the chairs; and finally the lot was gilt by Chatard.

The design of the backs of the chairs, with its cambered upper crosspiece, is also found on the four leaves of the folding screen. The original silk, provided by Desfarges in Lyons, has unfortunately been lost. The screen and the folding screen, together with twelve chairs, were acquired in 1793, at the revolutionary sales, by the upholsterer Marceau.

Jean-Baptiste-Claude Sené (1748–1803), master in 1769, became the chief purveyor to the Royal Household in 1785, thus eclipsing Boulard to a certain extent. He was the major beneficiary of the very large commissions given out at the eve of the Revolution for the furnishing of the royal apartments in Saint-Cloud, Fontainebleau, and Compiègne. But Sené also worked for private custom, as is attested by the furniture of the Salon Huet [198], which includes a sofa, two *bergères* (easy chairs) and eight armchairs, whose origins may finally be traced one day, thanks to their originality, costly materials, and workmanship.

We do, however, know about the origins of the two *voyeuses* (con-

Cassolette 'en Athénienne', *c.* 1780
Oak, carved, painted and gilt; chased and gilt bronze, patinated
1.050 x 0.420. Inv. 37

Jean-Baptiste Boulard (*c.* 1725–
1789), master in Paris in 1754
Folding screen, delivered in 1785 for
Louis XVI's Salon des Jeux in
Versailles
Beech, carved and gilt; leaves in
brocaded lampas representing rustic
scenes after Philippe de Lassalle
(1723–1805)
1.330 x 0.670 (each). Inv. 202

Jean-Baptiste Lelarge (1743–1802),
master in Paris in 1775
Screen, *c.* 1780
Limewood, beech, carved and gilt;
movable panel in brocaded lampas
representing a rustic scene after
Philippe de Lassalle
1.000 x 0.550. Inv. 652

Jean-Baptiste Claude Sené
(1748–1803), master in Paris
in 1769
Voyeuse (conversation chair),
delivered in 1789 for Madame
Elisabeth's Salon Turc in Montreuil
Beech, carved and painted
0.970 x 0.560 x 0.460. Inv. 70

versation chairs) [70] in the Grand Bureau, which were part of a
collection of four (a third is in the Musée des Arts Décoratifs).
They were commissioned in July 1789 for the Salon Turc, actually
the game room of Madame Elisabeth, the king's sister, in her
small Château de Montreuil in Versailles, and in all likelihood
delivered after the departure of the royal family for Paris. It can be
assumed that the princess did not have the opportunity of enjoying them, except perhaps during her infrequent visits during the
summer of 1790, when the court stayed at Saint-Cloud.
Conceived for a 'Turkish' drawing-room, these *voyeuses* do present
certain peculiarities in their decoration—crescent moons and
pearls—as well as in their shape; the sabre-legs appear to have
been inspired by those of the furniture which had already been
delivered by Jacob in 1777 for the Cabinet Turc of Count d'Artois
at the Temple (Musée du Louvre).
Sené was entrusted with the woodwork, but the carving was done
by Régnier who executed its festoons of pearls, sea-shells, cres-
cents, cloven feet, etc.; Chatard executed the painting in a grey
and white *réchampi*; finally Capin upholstered them with Jouy

Jean-Baptiste Claude Sené
(1748–1803), master in Paris in 1769
Bergère (easy chair), c. 1780
Beech, carved and gilt; upholstered
in 'petit point' tapestry
1.050 x 1.610 x 0.720. Inv. 198

Cartel clock, c. 1770–1780
Oak, limewood, carved and gilt
1.300 x 0.560. Inv. 25

cloth presenting a design of flowers and green palm-trees on a
white ground. The paint seems to have survived to this day, even
though it is thoroughly aged, but unfortunately the same does not
hold true of the fittings.

Gilt Bronze Furniture and Objets d'Art

As an indispensable feature of the furnishing of a luxurious eighteenth-century town-house, gilt bronze is handsomely represented in the Camondo collection: clocks, cartel clocks, barometers, fire-dogs, chandeliers, wall-lights, girandoles, vases were selected with as much care as the furniture proper. More care is called for today when it comes to attributing numerous works to the most famous bronze foundries such as Gouthière or Thomire; in the absence of signatures and marks, anonymity has only been par-

Clock 'with Chinaman', second half 18th century
Works by Sotiau, master in Paris in 1782
Chased, gilt, and patinated bronze, jade. 0.550 x 0.300 x 0.200. Inv. 182

Candelabra (detail), end 18th century
Chased and gilt bronze
1.040 x 0.420. Inv. 247

Pair of vases, *c.* 1740–1750
Chased and gilt bronze, blue
lacquered cardboard (?) imitating
chinaware. 0.200 x 0.100. Inv. 82

Candelabra, mid-18th century
Chased and gilt bronze
0.430 x 0.350. Inv. 209

Robert Osmond, master in Paris
in 1746
Cartel clock, *c.* 1775
Works by Hilgers, clock-maker, Paris
Chased and gilt bronze
0.860 x 0.440. Inv. 13

tially lifted by a few recent discoveries. Here again, one must note the very uneven balance between rococo and neo-classicism. Very few objects belong to the first of these two styles. The three girandoles of the Salon Huet [209], with their splendid scrolls, have, without any real proof, been linked with the production of François-Thomas Germain.

In the sphere of clock-making, two clocks deserve mention. The first, distinctly rocaille, with the statuette of a little girl in enamelled Sèvres biscuit-ware after Falconet, with a bronze terrace and a porcelain globe [152], rather brings to mind the knick-knacks sold by Lazare Duvaux or his colleagues. The other, in lacquered

Clock 'with a dead bird', *c.* 1780
Chased and gilt bronze, white and blue marble, diamonds
0.360 x 0.260 x 0.140. Inv. 671

Manufacture de Sèvres
Clock, *c.* 1750–1755
Works by Pothenot, Paris
Soft-paste porcelain, chased and gilt bronze. 0.310 x 0.230. Inv. 152

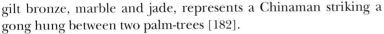

gilt bronze, marble and jade, represents a Chinaman striking a gong hung between two palm-trees [182].

The activities of the *marchands merciers* is also evoked by two curious vases [82], made out of some undefined material, lacquered cardboard or paste, in an imitation of Chinese turquoise-blue porcelain, whose rocaille fittings are none the less of excellent quality.

More numerous and more important are the clocks in transitional or Louis XVI style. Robert Osmond (*c.* 1720–1789), one of the few bronze founders who signed their work, left many objects that are profoundly marked by the transitional style. An outstanding cartel clock [13] acquired from Bensimon in 1934, bears his signature. Similar pieces were delivered in 1767 and 1770 to Madame Adélaïde and the dauphin in Versailles. On the mantelpiece of the Grand Bureau, an impressive patinated gilt bronze mantel clock [93], formerly in the Larcade collection and representing a satyr and a bacchante after Clodion, is the work of an unknown bronze founder. Nor do we know anything about the creator of the famous model of clocks 'with a dead bird' *('à l'oiseau mort')*, of which Marie-Antoinette and Count d'Artois both owned copies; the one in the count's room, with its double marble pedestal, has costly hands enhanced with cut diamonds [671].

Clock with bacchante and satyr,
c. 1780
Group after Clodion (1738–1814)
Works by Charles-Guillaume
Manière, master in Paris in 1778
Chased, gilt, and patinated bronze,
red and brown marble
0.750 x 0.500 x 0.210. Inv. 93

Clock in the shape of an obelisk,
c. 1765–1775
Works by Crosnier, Paris
Chased and gilt bronze, yellow
Sienna marble, blue, 'rouge royal',
and 'vert antique' marble
0.810 x 0.230 x 0.230. Inv. 606

Among the fire-dogs, one should mention a set of a sort that was fairly widespread, the ones with ornamental foliage and cupids, executed by Turpin after drawings by Forty. A set of this type was delivered in 1786 for the Salon des Nobles in Versailles; despite the hypothesis put forward by Pierre Verlet, it cannot be the one now in the Petit Bureau [373], since the latter's dimensions are too small.

Several remarkable chandeliers decorate Camondo's living quarters. The one in the dining room [245], an excellent instance of the 'Greek taste' or transitional style, has rightly been compared to certain drawings executed for Warsaw by Jean-Louis Prieur.

Recent research by Christian Baulez on the other hand, has revealed the provenance of the exceptional gilt bronze chandelier of the Grand Salon [146], acquired from Bauer in 1935. It is composed of a central vase and twelve arms held by three women whose upper body emerges from a cluster of acanthus leaves. Decorated with three satyr's heads, it may have originated from the Royal Household; in any event it was presented by Napoleon to Cambacérès, Arch-Chancellor of the Empire, in 1808 and graced his Parisian residence, now the Hôtel de Roquelaure. The chandelier may be attributed to François Rémond (c. 1745–1812), one of the most important bronze founders of his day, though paradoxically he is but little known. Master in 1774, he was the favourite supplier of the queen and of the Count d'Artois.

Chandelier, c. 1770
Chased and gilt bronze
0.920 x 0.870. Inv. 245

Jean-Noël Turpin, master in Paris in 1773
One of a pair of fire-dogs
Designed by Jean-François Forty
Chased and gilt bronze
0.300 x 0.370. Inv. 373

Among the numerous pairs of girandoles, or candelabras, those in the Grand Bureau [86] with their patinated bronze female figures stand out; they were acquired from Seligmann in 1925. Those of the dining room [247], bought at the same place in 1901, are remarkable by the abundance of their decoration: griffins, satyr's heads, amphoras suspended from chains, the lot being topped by six arms in the shape of hunting horns.

Equally deserving of interest are the numerous wall-lights. The set of eight of these spread through the entrance hall and the main staircase [12, 40], composed of female terms draped in the antique manner and bearing four candle-cups, correspond to the model created in 1766 by Jean-Louis Prieur for the royal palace in Warsaw.

In the dining room, four wall-lights with tree arms, rams' heads, garlands of laurel, and acanthus leaves [246], acquired from Seligmann in 1911, have judiciously been compared by Svend Eriksen with several deliveries made to the Royal Household about 1770

Wall-light, *c.* 1770–1780
Stamp of the Royal *Garde-Meuble*
Chased and gilt bronze
0.570 x 0.450. Inv. 246

Candelabra, *c.* 1780–1790
Chased, gilt, and patinated bronze,
red and brown marble
Height: 1.170. Inv. 86

Chandelier, end 18th century
Chased and gilt bronze
3.100 x 0.900. Inv. 146

by the *bronzier* Quentin-Claude Pitoin (*c.* 1725–1774). The Camondo wall-lights were inscribed with inventory numbers which are unfortunately difficult to decipher because they have been scratched out.

In the last third of the century, bronze played an increasingly important role in furniture, to the point that pieces of furniture even began to be made entirely out of metal. The Camondo Museum possesses three specimens of this kind.

The two silver-plated and gilt bronze consoles [190] in the Salon Huet, have traditionally been associated with those designed by Victor Louis in 1766 for the royal palace in Warsaw. But, as Svend Eriksen has shown, that particular model had already been described in an advertisement which the master locksmith Pierre Deumier placed in the *Avantcoureur* in 1763. Their production, if not their invention, can therefore be attributed to Deumier. The consoles, several other specimens of which are known to exist in various public and private collections, are a particularly precocious and masterful manifestation of the new interest in antiquity. On the other hand, no name has yet been attached to the sumptuous three-legged pedestal table in the Grand Salon [134] bought from Seligmann in 1900, which had until now been attributed, without proof, to Thomire. The table-top is borne by

three griffins, circled with a frieze of cupids bearing garlands.

The steel and gilt bronze bed dating from the very end of the eighteenth century, purchased from Lévy in 1913 and placed in Nissim de Camondo's room is equally anonymous [759]. Despite its thoroughly 'military' appearance, there is no good cause to suppose that it was turned out by the arms manufacture which Boutet had installed in the former Grand Commun of Versailles during the Revolution, since there is nothing to show that this establishment ever devoted itself to this sort of work, whose manner is rather reminiscent of certain Russian products.

Finally, Moïse de Camondo managed to assemble, with his infallible intuition, several curios whose provenances in some cases turned out to be prestigious. Nothing, to be sure, is known about the origins of the startling Japanese lacquer vase [144], whose gilt

Wall-light, *c.* 1765–1770
Chased and gilt bronze
0.720 x 0.750. Inv. 40

Console
Designed by Victor-Louis (1731–1795), delivered at the royal palace of Warsaw in 1766
Silver-plated and gilt bronze, green Egyptian marble
0.920 x 1.270 x 0.500. Inv. 190

Pedestal table, end 18th century
Chased and gilt bronze, Sarancolin marble. 0.790 x 0.650. Inv. 134

Vase, 2nd half 18th century
Japanese lacquer in a chased and
gilt bronze mount (*c.* 1780)
0.470 x 0.280. Inv. 144

Pair of covered vases, *c.* 1780
From the collections of Queen
Marie-Antoinette at Versailles
Chased and gilt bronze, petrified
wood. 0.430 x 0.180. Inv. 153

bronze mount with sphinxes and foliage, strike one as the work of
a most talented jeweller. Who created it, and what *marchand mercier*, with the possible exception of a Daguerre, could have offered
this refined object to the most demanding of his customers?
Thanks to the perspicacity of Christian Baulez on the other hand,
we now know all about the provenance of the precious pair of
vases carved out of petrified wood, around which are entwined
finely chased gilt bronze serpents. Until the first days of the
Revolution they decorated the 'cabinets intérieurs' of the queen
at Versailles. But justifiably worried at the impending storm, on 10
October 1789, she entrusted her collections of precious objects to
Daguerre. On 16 November 1793, shortly after the death of Marie-
Antoinette, the latter, in agreement with his associate Lignereux,
returned the whole lot to the Nation. On this occasion, a most
accurate description was made of the vases. They could be traced
back with certainty to July 1798, when, somewhat ironically, the
Directoire put them up for sale, with other royal objects, to cover
the expenses attending upon the installation of the *Muséum.* They
were to reappear in 1841, at the Baron Rogé sale, before becoming one of the jewels of Moïse de Camondo's collection.

The room of Nissim de Camondo
(1892–1917)
Bed, *c.* 1790–1795
Steel and gilt bronze
1.080 x 2.130 x 1.260. Inv. 759
Carolus-Duran (1837–1917)
*Portrait of Nissim de Camondo
(1830–1889)*, 1882
Oil on canvas, 1.270 x 0.950. Inv. 765

Silverware

The collection of French silverware assembled by Count Moïse de Camondo is significant not so much in quantity as in its exceptional quality and the distinguished provenance of its finest pieces. The museum catalogue devotes nineteen entries to silver; in fact, there are more objects than that, since several of them come in pairs.

It is obvious that Moïse de Camondo did not intend to create a collection whose variety and encyclopaedic scope might have invited comparison with the great museum collections which were then being assembled at the Louvre or the Musée des Arts Décoratifs. Quite to the contrary, his chief concern seems to have been to round off his own idea of a wealthy French home of the end of the eighteenth century by the logical inclusion of sumptuous table silver, along with various other objects including several pairs of candlesticks.

The acquisitions focused chiefly on the Parisian production before the Revolution. Only one provincial item is to be seen: a taster from the Riom region, dating from 1775–1781 [325], and only one set of silverware is posterior to the Ancien Régime: the set of vermeil cutlery produced by Pierre-Joseph Dehanne between 1809 and 1819 [286].

One relatively coherent group of objects is remarkable for its provenance: it includes the three pairs of candlesticks by Besnier [375], Soulaine [97], and Ménière [98], the first two having formerly belonged to the collection of Baron Pichon while the third was part of the Double collection. All three subsequently entered the collection of Count Isaac de Camondo, who bequeathed them, at his death in 1911, to his first cousin Moïse. Incidentally, the Isaac de Camondo collection, accepted by the Louvre in 1911, included both a prestigious selection of paintings, and a very fine collection of French eighteenth-century furniture and objets d'art. Among the silverware there was a famous *flambeau de bureau* by Thomas Germain as well as a tureen by Antoine-Jan de Villeclair.

We do not know the circumstances in which certain relatively modest objects were acquired by Moïse de Camondo; this is the case of the two Parisian goblets by Jacques Famechon, done in 1777/78 [275], and of another made by François Corbie in 1781/82 [274]. We do know, however, that the two tasters, the aforementioned one from Riom and the other by an unidentified Parisian master done about 1756–1762 [276], were acquired in 1916. The twelve little vermeil goblets by René-Pierre Ferrier, made in 1789 [280], were bought in 1922 from Boivin. Furthermore, the two silver and blue crystal sugar bowls made by Noël

The Dining Room
The wainscot in green *réchampi* is partly 18th-century. On the table is the silver *pot à oille* by Auguste.

Piton in 1776–1778 [281] were added to the Museum's collection in 1924.

After these relatively modest beginnings, the acquisitions became more spectacular and more frequent. First came the acquisition, in 1928, of the *pot à oille* made by Auguste in 1784/85 [254]. Starting in 1929, and thanks to the assistance of the antique dealer Jacques Helft, Moïse de Camondo was able to buy the magnificent vestiges of the Russian court, dispersed by the Soviet government towards the end of the twenties.

First came the two rectangular compotiers complete with their lids, made by Robert-Joseph Auguste, followed the next year by

Jacques Besnier (*c.* 1698–1761),
master in Paris in 1720
Pair of candlesticks, 1719/20
Silver. 0.257 x 0.151. Inv. 375

another pair, square in shape [256–257]—the lot, dated 1782/83, was one of the pieces commissioned by Empress Catherine II. In 1930, Helft sold the count the two candlesticks by François-Thomas Germain, made in 1762, whose provenance remains enigmatic [216].

An even more spectacular purchase was made in 1933, again through Jacques Helft, of items from the table set which Catherine II offered Gregory Orloff: the four wine buckets and one of the *pots à oille* [253–255]; the second one was acquired the following year. The tureen from the same service [252] was also purchased in 1934, but now at Bensimon's.

The collection of silverware assembled by Moïse de Camondo does not claim to provide a complete overview of French production in the eighteenthy century, particularly since most of the items—and indeed the most significant among them—belong to the second half of that century. Still, the Regency is well represented by two candlesticks from 1719–1720 made by Jacques Besnier, and whose markedly architectural character attests to the durability of the still strongly perceptible classical style. The very shallow chasing, mosaic background, interlacing, palmettos, fleurons, and rosettes combine harmoniously with cast ornaments: female mascarons, pilasters, or masks of satyrs. The two-light candle-holders that go with it, bear the stamp of Martin Berthe; they were produced somewhat earlier, *c.* 1714/15. Unfortunately, we do not know at what point the four objects were brought together.

Dating from 1726/27, the candlesticks by Soulaine belong to the first years of Louis XV's reign. The Regency style is still apparent in the greater part of the ornamentation—shells, satyr's masks, interlacings, palmettos, female mascarons—but their livelier silhouette is already rococo.

François-Thomas Germain was the last representative of a powerful and prestigious dynasty of goldsmiths, three generations of which had followed one another in the Galleries of the Louvre at the service of Louis XIV and later of Louis XV. Born in 1726, he succeeded his father, Thomas, who had trained him, in 1748. All seemed to forebode a splendid career, unmarked by anxiety, and

Paul Soulaine (?-1759), master in Paris in 1720
Pair of candlesticks, 1726–1727
Silver. 0.234 x 0.156. Inv. 97

Germain did indeed show a prodigious activity at the service of the most brilliant courts of Europe—Versailles, Lisbon, St Petersburg—for over 17 years. Unfortunately, fate, a carefree spirit and the malevolence that pursued him led to the destruction of his prestigious workshop in 1765: Germain went bankrupt and was obliged to give up his splendid situation for good.

His production, spread out between the years 1748 and 1765, shows a broad and very definite fidelity to rococo ornament. Yet, already at the beginning of the 1760s, Germain sometimes rather successfully adopted the new manner marked by the apparition of neo-classicism. The two candlesticks of the Camondo Museum are attractive instances of this: the architectonic structure and 'antique' ornamentation with heavy garlands of laurel, clearly reflect the influence of engravings by Delafosse or Lorrain. The three towers placed at the base of the candle-holder have led to an intriguing hypothesis concerning the provenance of these candlesticks: it has been suggested that they were the emblem of Madame de Pompadour. The towers would, in that case, be an allusion to those that appear in the arms of the marquise. However, it should be remembered that items of silverware decorated with towers were also made by Germain for the court of Portugal. To judge from their proportions, these candlesticks must have been conceived for a dressing table; indeed, they are rather reminiscent of those belonging to the dressing table made by Germain in 1765 for the princess of Portugal, the future Maria I.

The silversmith with the largest number of works in the Camondo Museum is undoubtedly Jacques-Nicolas Roettiers. His family came from Antwerp and he was the son of Jacques Roettiers, silversmith to the king in the Galleries of the Louvre. He, too, benefited from an exceptional training in his father's workshop. He became a master silversmith in Paris in 1765, and thereafter

Jean-Nicolas Ménière, master
in Paris in 1770
Candlestick, 1771/72
Silver. 0.270 x 0.143. Inv. 98

François-Thomas Germain
(1726–1791), master in Paris in 1748
Candlestick, 1762
Silver gilt. 0.173 x 0.112. Inv. 216

Jacques-Nicolas Roettiers de La Tour
(1736–after 1784), master in Paris
in 1765
Tureen and tray commissioned by
Catherine II for Gregory Orloff,
1770/71
Silver. 0.270 x 0.415 x 0.260
(tureen) ; 0.493 x 0.434 (tray)
Inv. 252

assisted his father in his capacity of 'orfèvre ordinaire du Roi' (silversmith in ordinary). He did a lot of work for the French royal family, but his most ambitious creations were done for the Russian court. It was in the course of the year 1770 that Catherine II commissioned Roettiers father and son to make an enormous silver table set which she intended to offer her favourite Gregory Orloff. Roettiers delivered his work in the years 1771/72. In 1907, the set of exceptional importance included 842 items of French workmanship; home-produced items were later added to it. At the death of Orloff, in 1783, Catherine II bought the whole lot back from his heirs. The table set remained in the imperial collections

Jacques-Nicolas Roettiers de La Tour
(1736–after 1784),
master in Paris in 1765
Pot à oille with tray and wine bucket
commissioned by Catherine II for
Gregory Orloff, 1770/71
Silver. 0.263 x 0.393 x 0.273
(tureen) ; 0.490 (tray) ; 0.264
x 0.258 x 0.190 (bucket)
Inv. 253, 255

until the Revolution. Shortly before 1930, parts of it were dispersed ; besides what has remained in Leningrad and Moscow, scattered elements are to be found today in numerous public and private collections throughout the world : the Louvre, the Metropolitan Museum, etc.

In 1907, the set included twenty-two *soupières* (soup tureens), though it cannot exactly be established how many of these were *pots à oille*, which are round, and tureens, which are oval. Except for this sole difference, the two forms are very similar, with four feet in the shape of consoles providing a powerful support for the ample form of the bowl. The ornamentation with its monumental scale consists exclusively of classical motifs: piasters, laurel branches, gadroons, interlace, and acanthus leaves.

The wine buckets, of which it seems there were sixteen in 1907, are markedly inspired by antique vases; they are vigorously ornamented with gadroons, fluting, beads, and laurels, and circled about the middle with festoons of ivy, the emblem of Bacchus.

With its ample and powerful style, the Orloff silver is generally considered to be one of the first manifestations of neo-classicism in silverware. But Roettiers seems to have drawn inspiration not only from models of antiquity, but also, more surprisingly, from the large pieces of silverware of Louis XIV, and more specifically from the silver furnishings of Versailles, molten down in 1690, of which numerous graphic representations subsist. Indeed, this is not the only instance of such a display of nostalgia for Louis XIV style during the years between 1760 and 1770.

Although a similar phenomenon is encountered in both architecture and furniture, its impact on the psychological mood that gave birth to neo-classicism has hardly received any attention.

Neo-classicism only attained its utmost perfection in the work of Robert-Joseph Auguste. Born in Mons in 1723, Auguste belonged to none of the prestigious lines of 'royal' goldsmiths, but his career raised him to the front ranks.

Having already obtained his mastership in Paris in 1757, he was granted the title of 'orfèvre ordinaire du Roi' in 1778. The closing down of Germain's workshop in 1765 and the premature retirement of Roettiers in 1777 opened the way to him. Installed in the Galleries of the Louvre in 1784, he enjoyed a solid international reputation, and simultaneously served the courts of Lisbon, London, Copenhagen, Stockholm, and St Petersburg, where Empress Catherine II began calling upon his services in 1778.

An endless flow of abundant commissions led to the creation of various sets of tableware that were subsequently given the names of several cities of the empire: Ekaterinoslav, Nizhny-Novogorod, Kazan, and Moscow, although the question of distinguishing them with any certainty remains problematical. As with the Orloff set,

Robert-Joseph Auguste (1723–?), master in Paris in 1757
Pair of square compotiers with covers, executed for Catherine II, 1782/83
Silver. 0.032 x 0.270 (compotiers); 0.155 x 0.248 (covers). Inv. 257

the soviet sales in the interwar years led to the dispersion of parts of these sets. It is generally assumed that the four dishes or compotiers together with their dish-covers, now in the Camondo Museum, were part of the so-called Moscow set, completed in 1782/83.

The compotiers are edged with a laurel torus. The dish-covers rest on a plain rim surmounted with a gadroon. Above this unfolds a broad frieze of flutes and darts on a matted ground. They are crowned with a rosette of acanthus leaves round a core in the shape of a fir-cone. A dish-cover with the same design, and no doubt originating from the same set is now in the collection of the Musée des Arts Décoratifs. A similar model, with very slight modifications, is to be found in the dish-covers of the set Auguste supplied to the king of England, George III, also in 1783/84.

Robert Joseph Auguste (1723–?),
master in Paris in 1757
Pot à oille and tray, 1784–1789
Unidentified Parisian, master
Ladle, 1785–1786
Silver. 0.312 x 0.360 x 0.275 (pot à
oille) ; 0.309 (tray) ; 0.433 x 0.079
(ladle). Inv. 254

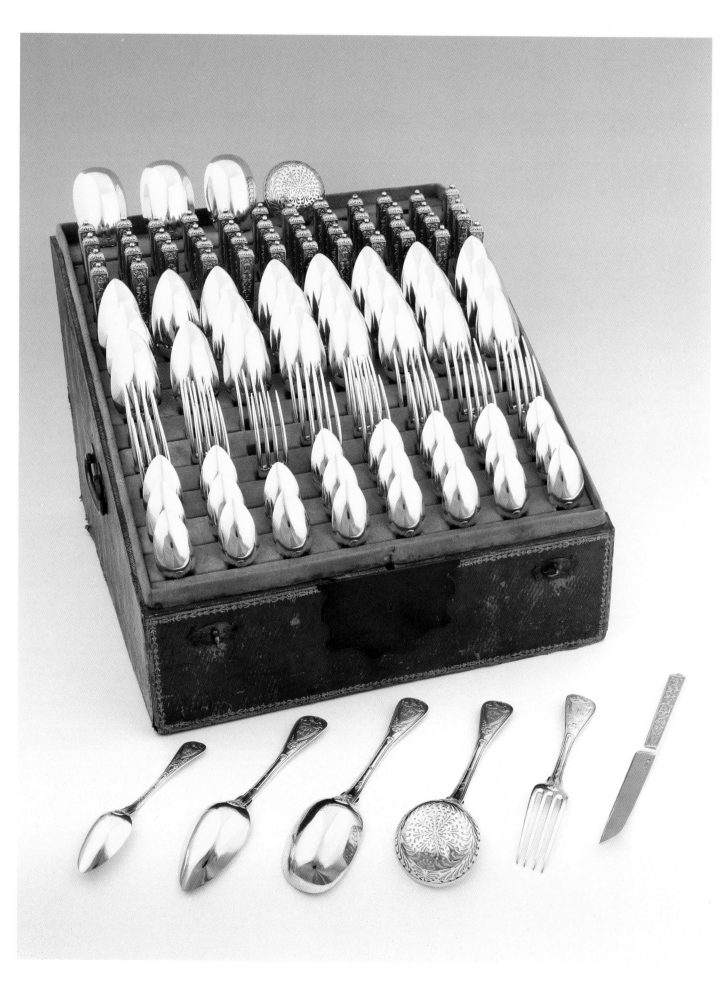

Though it was made one year after the foregoing set, the *pot à oille* by Auguste in the Camondo Museum is strikingly more archaic in style. Its provenance is unknown, but the coat of arms shows it was bought by a foreign—perhaps a Portuguese—customer. The ample, bellied shape, the foliated ornamentation, the swelling lid in the form of a cyma, surmounted with a highly naturalistic wild boar's head, and the beautifully worked plate are ever so much stylistic factors demonstrating the belated survival of rocaille at that date. The splendid ladle, which is elegantly chased with scallop-shells, does not, however, appear to be the work of Auguste.

Noël Piton, master in Paris in 1758
Sugar bowl and tray, 1776–1778
Silver, blue crystal
0.150 x 0.160 x 0.101 (bowl) ;
0.206 (tray). Inv. 281

Pierre Joseph Dehanne
Dessert set, 1809–1819
Vermeil. Inv. 286

Porcelain

The collection of porcelain assembled by Moïse de Camondo cannot claim to rival those found in other museums, at Sèvres, the Louvre, or the Musée des Arts Décoratifs; nor had he intended to gather coherent and exhaustive series, but rather to restore to this technique the position it held, during the eighteenth century in any elegant and aristocratic dwelling.

The passion of Louis-Henri, Duke of Bourbon (1692–1740) for oriental porcelain, was the original cause of the celebrity of the Manufacture de Chantilly. Founded about 1725, its prime vocation had been the imitation of oriental models. Its production was confined to soft-paste porcelain, executed without kaolin. Until

Manufacture de Chantilly
Pair of glass coolers, *c.* 1735
Soft-paste porcelain with Kakiemon decoration, chased and gilt bronze. 0.101 x 0.125. Inv. 391

about 1750, under the direction of Sicaire Cirou, Chantilly craftsmen were highly successful in copying Japanese 'Kakiemon' decoration. This ware—still the most sought-after Chantilly product—is rather well represented at the Camondo Museum by two pairs of glass coolers, with gilt bronze mounts [390, 391], two cylindrical bottles, two four-lobed sugar-bowls on a tray, and a mustard pot [288]. After Cirou died in 1751, the oriental inspiration gave way to a European style essentially characterized by polychrome and naturalistic floral designs. The various series of plates displayed in the Cabinet des Porcelaines belong to this period [289, 290]. After 1760, Chantilly produced cheaper items, though not devoid of charm, simply decorated in blue camaïeu, such as the carnation motif, which is displayed in the gallery, in a fine selection of plates and compotiers [317].

Manufacture de Vincennes
Covered milk goblet and saucer, 1753
Soft-paste porcelain, sky-blue ground. 0.140 x 0.200 (goblet); 0.205 (saucer). Inv. 392

Meissen manufacture
Tea-pot on heater, tea-pot, tea-box,
cup, sugar pot, *c.* 1750
Hard-paste porcelain. Inv. 295–296

At a time when French porcelain makers did not know about kaolin and had not mastered the production of hard-paste porcelain—although they managed, with true ingenuity and thanks to considerable technical prowess, to imitate its appearance—the factory of Meissen in Saxony had perfectly mastered the art of producing 'true' porcelain thanks to discoveries made by Böttger as early as 1708. From the purely artistic point of view, both French soft-paste porcelain and German hard-paste porcelain had attained the heights of perfection. The mid-eighteenth-century activity at Meissen is represented in the Museum's collection by tea and coffee sets [295, 296] and various items of tableware [298, 299, 300], decorated with multi-coloured birds, on a ground of violet-rose imbrications.

The Manufacture de Vincennes, founded in 1738 to compete with Meissen, managed to eclipse its French rivals, Saint-Cloud, Chantilly, and Mennecy. All of these, and Vincennes among them, were to distinguish themselves in the production of soft-paste porcelain. The king's increasing interest, encouraged by Madame de Pompadour, assured the latter an exceptional development.

The Camondo Museum is not rich in Vincennes ware, but three objects deserving of interest should none the less be mentioned. Two groups in enamelled biscuit-ware, the *Bird Hunter* and the

Manufacture de Vincennes
The Hare Hunter and *The Bird Hunter*,
1745–1750
Enamelled soft-paste porcelain,
chased and gilt bronze
0.150 x 0.240. Inv. 389

Hare Hunter [389], correspond to two models of which the first specimens were sold in 1752; their designer has not yet been identified.

The remarkable quality of its decoration and gilding also draws one's attention to a two-handled milk goblet and its saucer (1753) [392], with a sky-blue ground, ornamented with flowers.

In 1756, the manufacture moved from Vincennes to Sèvres, where it has remained to this day. This move did not lead to any interruption in the establishment's production and it definitively became the king's property in 1760. The brilliance of the manufacture's coloured grounds, the quality of its painted and gilt ornamentation, and the diversity of forms constantly gained in assurance. Even after the development of hard paste in 1769, soft-paste porcelain maintained its primacy.

It was in 1899 that Moïse de Camondo bought the rare pair of three-branched Sèvres wall-lights, in lapis lazuli *(bleu lapis)* and gold, from Seligmann. They are to be seen in the Salon Huet [217]. This stunningly daring model was created about 1760 by Jean-Claude Duplessis. Between 1761 and 1768, the factory sold about twenty pairs, including ten to the king, and a number of others to tradesmen like Poirier and to private customers. Madame de Pompadour owned two pairs, including a pink, blue, and green one that is now in the Louvre. A total of only six pairs of 'Duplessis mantelpiece lights' are known to exist today. Also produced by Sèvres is a water jug and oval basin (1765) with relief decoration *('Roussel à reliefs')*, a green ground, and landscapes enlivened with birds by François Aloncle [393].

In the Cabinet des Porcelaines the visitor may admire the famous *Service aux Oiseaux*, whose beauty, charm, and poetic quality admirably embody the talent and genius of the Manufacture.

Starting at the middle of the eighteenth century, when taste became marked by an increasing naturalism, birds were given a favoured place in the painted decoration of various centres, whether hard-paste porcelain (Meissen), soft-paste porcelain (Chantilly, Mennecy, Vincennes, and later Sèvres), or in *petit feu* faience (Sceaux, Aprey, or Rouen). In comparison to the highly stylized oriental ornamentation, these European items stand out by their manifest realism, although these birds, shown either on the ground, in flight, or poised on a branch, in rather repetitive attitudes, are pure creatures of the imagination, and hardly ever correspond to any species that can actually be identified.

These motifs were to be entirely renewed after the publication of *Histoire naturelle des oiseaux*, by Georges-Louis Leclerc, Count de Buffon (1707–1788), between 1770 and 1783. It would appear that it was at Sèvres that somebody first thought of transposing onto porcelain the endless variety of birds represented in the numerous plates inserted into Buffon's monumental opus. The unlimited number of items composing a table set provided an ideal base for an encyclopaedic development of this kind. In fact, thanks to the archives of the Manufacture de Sèvres one can establish a list of the different 'ornithological' sets, usually referred to as the 'services Buffon', produced during the reign of Louis XVI. Not only did the representation of the various species attempt to follow Buffon's illustrations as accurately as possible, but care was taken to inscribe the exact names of the birds on the back of the dish.

The first of these sets was acquired in 1782 by the Count d'Artois. Executed between 1779 and 1784, edged in green and gold, this set, at the time of the first delivery in 1782, included 177 items, four of which—a *verrière* and three glass coolers—are now at the Louvre.

In 1782, the Duke of Chartres (who would later be known as Philippe-Egalité), ordered a second set of 'Buffon' ware with an *œil-de-perdrix* border on a sky-blue ground, and birds in oval reserves, which he was to present to Nathaniel Parker Forth. The set, executed between 1782 and 1786, is now in an English private collection.

In 1784, the Manufacture was working on another set with birds by Buffon, as can be seen from a letter the director wrote to Count d'Angiviller on 27 March. The set with a 'pointillé ground and

Manufacture de Sèvres
Water jug and basin. Decorated by
François Aloncle (active between
1758 and 1781), 1765
Soft-paste porcelain, green ground
0.200 (jug) ; 0.090 x 0.300 x 0.230
(basin). Inv. 393

Manufacture de Sèvres
Wall-light, *c.* 1760
Soft-paste porcelain
0.450 x 0.310. Inv. 217

antique heads', was destined to a certain Le Fevre, a merchant in Amsterdam, who received it in December 1784. It appears plausible that the items that emerged in 1881 at the sale of the belongings of Baron Leopold Double, and which are now to be seen in the Cabinet des Porcelaines [293], represent a substantial part of this service. It has a green ground with black and gold *œils-de-perdrix*; also, the raised rims of the plates and the faces of the various items are decorated with birds in rectangular reserves and with grey camaïeu medallions containing antique profiles. Since most of the pieces bear the marks of the years 1784 and 1786, the service was completed at a later date. Made of soft paste,

Manufacture de Sèvres
Items of the so-called 'Buffon' set
Square compotier, oval compotier,
deep plate, dinner plate, 1784
Soft-paste porcelain. Inv. 292–293

it includes deep and dinner plates, oval, square or shell-shaped compotiers, a pair of oval sugar bowls, a pair of ice buckets, a pair of oval butter dishes, two trays with a pair of jam pots each, along with egg cups and various other items. The marks of several painters can be recognized: Dutanda, Philippine the Elder, Taillandier, Vieillard.

In March 1787, the Manufacture delivered a Buffon service to Count de Montmorin, the Minister of Foreign Affairs; it was intended to be presented to William Eden, the English ambassador, during the productive negotiations of the 1787 trade treaty. This set, with its black and gold *œils-de-perdrix* border on a green ground, is very similar to the foregoing; it was not as luxurious however, to the extent that the raised rims present neither ca-

Manufacture de Sèvres
Items of the so-called 'Buffon' set
Hard-paste porcelain: ice bucket,
tea-pot (1785), round sugar bowl
(1785)
Soft-paste porcelain: oval sugar bowl
(1784), tray with a pair of jam pots
(1784), two double salt cellars, two
ice cups (1784), egg cup, salt cellar
(1786). Inv. 292–293

maïeu medallions, nor birds in reserves. It was presumably completed at a later date and has since been dispersed. A batch of 93 items, dated between 1784 and 1788, were sold at auctions in London and New York in 1975 and 1977, and now belong to a British private collection. Another important part of the Eden set, acquired by Moïse de Camondo [292, 258], has been added to the Le Fevre set in the Cabinet des Porcelaines. This second set includes soft-paste items: deep plates and dinner plates (1784), butter dishes (1793), glass-coolers (1784–1786), ice cups (1784), sauce-boats with two spouts, radish dishes, a mortar (1788), oil cruets (1786), salt cellars, etc. Among the hard-paste items are two slightly different pairs of four-footed round bowls, or ice-cups (?) (1788), after the model by Louis Le Masson, two sauce-boats in the shape of an antique lamp (1793), a large square compotier, four oval tureens (1793), and finally a circular basin dated 1804–1809. These items also bear the marks of various painters: Dodin, Gérard, Levé *père*, Massy, Mérault, Moiron, Rosset, etc. It is not quite certain, however, that the later pieces really belonged to the Eden set.

A cabaret including a tea-pot, sugar-bowl, milk-pot (hard paste) and a cup (soft paste), made in 1785–1788, with a similar decoration, was also acquired by Count de Camondo [294]. As can be seen, the Buffon set assembled by Camondo is far from being homogeneous, and includes items from various sources, purchased on several occasions before 1911, from various antique dealers, among which Seligmann and Stettiner.

It should be added that Sèvres created one last Buffon service during the revolutionary period. It had a yellow raised rim touched up with black. Some pieces of it are now to be found in the Musée des Arts Décoratifs. Other manufactures adopted the formula, such as Tournai, working for the Duke of Orléans (in the royal collections in England) in 1787, or again, in the early part of the nineteenth century, the Dagoty brothers, working for the Duke of Padua (private collection).

The discovery of limousin kaolin at Saint-Yrieix, in 1765, soon allowed France to produce hard-paste porcelain, to which certain Parisian and provincial manufactures devoted themselves exclusively after 1770. This was the case of the manufacture of Niderviller in Lorraine, founded in 1754, and bought back in 1770 by Count de Custine, who gave it a powerful impetus, as witness the beauty and quality of the garniture Moïse de Camondo acquired from Seligmann in 1897 [100]. The set is composed of three vases after the antique, the largest of which is a clock with a revolving dial signed by Arnoud *père*, a clock-maker from Nancy. On a lapis lazuli ground, strewn with golden flowers, magnificent garlands of white biscuit flowers have been applied, revealing a dazzling virtuosity. Polychrome landscapes (on the clock), and oval medallions representing children's games in grey camaïeu (on the vases), complete the decoration of these three items, in which the austerity of neo-classicism is harmoniously inflected by the most delicate naturalistic sensibility.

Manufacture de Niderviller
Garniture: clock with two vases,
c. 1785
Heights: 0.360, 0.340. Inv. 100

Carpets and Tapestries

Count Moïse de Camondo took particular care to assemble a collection of furniture and objects of the eighteenth century. His love for things both rare and of high quality is also apparent in the collection of Savonnerie carpets which were destined to be placed in the various rooms of his town-house. His choice went to the more spectacular production of this manufacture, and several of the items he acquired originally belonged to the royal collection. The finest piece is undoubtedly the carpet in the Salon Doré [176] since it was part of the set commissioned by Louis XIV for the Grande Galerie of the Louvre which is four hundred metres long and nine wide. Ninety-three carpets (one of which was never

Manufacture de la Savonnerie
Carpet, *c.* 1678
Wool. 5.150 x 4.340. Inv. 176

Manufacture de la Savonnerie
Carpet, *c.* 1740
Wool. 6.000 x 5.700. Inv. 234

made) were to be woven for its decoration. Certain carpets were duplicated to be presented to foreign princes, so that no less than 104 carpets came off the looms between 1671 and 1688.

Some of them are decorated with the royal attributes, others with allegorical figures representing Water, Air, Courage, or Glory ... The *Allegory of Air* of the Salon Doré was the fiftieth of the series. J. Guiffrey's description in the general inventory of the royal furniture under Louis XIV reveals that this central part, decorated with four heads representing the winds blowing into trumpets, was completed at either end by two low-reliefs with a blue ground on which stood out the figures of Aeolus and of Juno.

The two parts, assembled into a single item, were sold by Sotheby Parke Bernet in Monaco on 4 December 1983.

Manufacture de la Savonnerie
Portière, c. 1680–1690
Wool. 4.100 x 3.070. Inv. 333

Manufacture de la Savonnerie
Carpet, c. 1678 (detail)
Wool. 5.150 x 4.340. inv. 176

In view of their size, one may well understand that these carpets were cut into smaller pieces and occasionally adapted to the decoration of a salon. Over the years, certain items stored in the warehouse were subjected, from one regime to the next, to various modifications. Such is the case of a carpet [234] in which the fleurs-de-lis of the central part were erased during the Revolution, preserving only the necklaces of St Michael and of the Holy Spirit topped with a crown and bearing two white wings around the shield.

With its ornamental foliage, garlands of flowers, volutes, cornucopiae, and the intensity of the colours, it bears comparison with certain carpets executed for the Royal Household, particularly that of the Fontainebleau chapel. This series was designed by Jacques Perrot, who worked for the manufacture from 1725 to 1750.

Certain carpets, having been approved by the king, were woven a second time, so, for instance, the one intended for the Chambre du Comte [721], delivered on 4 March 1760 for the religious service of Mesdames de France, on Sundays and holidays, at the chapel of Versailles. The first model was made in 1745 and woven for the third time in 1766.

The Manufacture de la Savonnerie did not restrict itself to weaving carpets, and its production included table covers, seat covers and *portières*, one specimen of which [333] is now in the collections of the Museum. A trophy composed of a lion with armour and standards appears on a black ground. In the upper part a sun is framed with the motto of Louis XIV 'Nec pluribus impar'. Three other hangings of this kind are to be found, one in the Ephrussi Rothschild Museum at Saint-Jean-Cap-Ferrat, while two others are owned by private collectors.

Because of its extremely sturdy weave, the Savonnerie products provided an ideal covering for seats. Two carved beech armchairs [38], formerly in the castle of La Roche-Guyon, are upholstered with tapestry representing large polychrome bouquets. Two other armchairs of the same series are to be found in the Metropolitan Museum in New York.

One carpet [177] presents a problem. Its shape, and above all its floral composition suggests that it was intended as a table cover. The central motif, in the shape of a crown, is framed by a frieze and no doubt covered the table top, while the border on which a garland of flowers alternates with vases and baskets, and a bouquet tied with a blue ribbon at each one of the four corners, would have hung vertically. This hypothesis is confirmed by comparing this item with others of the same type (Metropolitan Museum, Waddesdon Manor). Even if the dimensions are different, the same principle governs the arrangement of the motifs, some of which are intended to be viewed vertically.

Two other carpets [177–178] are *dessus-de-banquettes*. One of these [178] covered a seat delivered, in 1745, for the apartments of the dauphin and dauphine in Fontainebleau (second antechamber). The same model, decorated with a head of Apollo with ornamental foliage and garlands of flowers was delivered two years later to Versailles. In addition to the one in the Camondo Museum, two other such items are known to exist, one in the Mobilier National, another at Waddesdon Manor. All these attributions have

been made thanks to the research undertaken by Pierre Verlet on the basis of the archives of the Duvivier family which, between 1715 and 1826, occupied various positions, including that of director of the Savonnerie manufacture.

Folding screens were an important element of interior decoration at that period; they made the rooms cozier and compensated for the inadequacies of the heating. Documentary evidence already reveals the existence of Savonnerie folding screens in 1707. Three artists, Blain de Fontenay, Audran, and Desportes, acquired a reputation designing compositions for these screens, the latter executing scenes with animals to decorate them. The

Museum's collections include a folding screen that belonged to the Duvivier family [141]. This exceptional item still has its old arrangement in the form of two-faced panels, a presentation that would subsequently be replaced by an obverse covered with crimson cloth.

The six double panels are divided thus:
1. Singerie in rocaille style (painted sketch, Manufacture de Sèvres);
2. Bird of prey in a frame of cornucopiae and flowery trellis-work;
3. Eagle owl perched on a poppy tuft, surrounded with birds (subject drawn from one of Aesop's fables *The owl and the birds*; the composition may be compared with that of the first fountain of the labyrinth in the gardens of Versailles);
4. Bird of prey attacking ducks; same frame as 2;
5. Cockatoo perched on a rosebush, flight of birds, same as 1;
6. Flight of birds, same as 2.

In view of their success, each panel was redone many times over. Over a hundred were woven between 1719 and 1738. The animal scenes are quite similar in each case, and only the decorative elements were subject to minor modifications.

Armorial tapestries *(chancelleries)* were intended as presents which the king offered the high chancellor. The one presented in the hall of the Museum [45] displays the arms of France upheld by two winged figures on a fleur-de-lis ground and, on the border, the

Manufacture de la Savonnerie
Armchair, *c.* 1725–1730
Beech, carved; upholstered in wool
1.090 x 0.700 x 0.630. Inv. 38

Manufacture de la Savonnerie
Carpet, *c.* 1680
Wool. 2.550 x 2.800. Inv. 177

Manufacture de la Savonnerie
Folding screen, *c.* 1735–1740
Wool. 1.370 x 0.630 (each panel)
Inv. 141

Manufacture des Gobelins
Chancellerie, *c.* 1680
Wool, silk. 3.500 x 3.600. Inv. 45

royal monogram in crowned escutcheons. The arms at the corners are those of Chancellor d'Argenson (1652–1721) who was born in Venice at the time his father Count d'Argenson, was ambassador there. He had been made knight protector of St Marc on 15 January 1653, which accounts for the presence of the arms of Venice in his escutcheon.

This *chancellerie* had formerly belonged to Michel le Tellier and it is believed to have been drawn by Claude III Audran. Its provenance seems to be confirmed by a note dated 1747, drawing up the list of the *chancelleries* executed upon the orders of the Duke d'Antin, in which it is specified that d'Argenson, ten years earlier, had entrusted Audran with the task of changing the corners of five or six items belonging to Monseigneur le Tellier and 'that in view of the craftsmanship, these items were made in Brussels'. This identification is plausible. For if we compare the central motif of this tapestry with a drawing by Audran now in the Nationalmuseum in Stockholm, it becomes obvious that this

Screen, *c.* 1760
Limewood, carved and gilt. Leaf in Gobelins tapestry representing cupids with flowers and birds after François Boucher (1703–1770)
1.170 x 0.780. Inv. 203

Manufacture des Gobelins
Portière, *c.* 1775
After a cartoon by Charles Tessier
Wool, silk. 3.070 x 1.440. Inv. 232

chancellerie is indeed the one in the Camondo Museum.

The Manufacture des Gobelins is represented by two panels from a screen [203–204] decorated with cupids, flowers, and birds after Boucher; one of them bears the mark of J. Neilson, director of the low-warp workshops from 1760 to 1783. The painter Tessier had executed drawings for the *Don Quixote* series after Coypel.

In 1760, Jacques executed a painting of a red damask cloth which was to serve as a model for some *portières* assorted to this hanging. Those of the Salon Huet [232] are decorated with garlands and crowns of flowers bound with a blue ribbon.

Several still lifes in the Museum's collections illustrate the infatuation for this type of composition. They were woven after the paintings of Anne Vallayer-Coster (1744–1818). She was noted for her talent while she was still very young and praised by Diderot and Bachaumont. She was admitted to the Académie Royale de Peinture in 1770, and Jean-Baptiste Pierre was a fervent admirer and friend. Pierre became administrator of the Gobelins in 1781, and it was no doubt on his initiative that the works of Vallayer-Coster were woven into tapestries.

Marianne Roland-Michel has published an inventory of the paintings which served as models at the Gobelins and Savonnerie manufactures. The vase with a dead bird [621] and the vase with

flowers and plums [622] were woven in the early nineteenth century on the basis of paintings exhibited in the Salons of 1781 and 1798. Executed after two paintings dating from 1766, *The Brioche* or *The Breakfast* [265] and its pendant, *Le Service à Crème* or *The Dessert*, reveal a talent for composition in the juxtaposition of the most modest objects. These two tapestries are marked with a stamp bearing the royal arms, and were presented, in 1814, by the administrator of the Gobelins, to the Duchess of Angoulême, who had been charmed by their freshness. Two other still lifes [620], produced at the Savonnerie, are now in the Museum's collections. They belonged to the Marquess of Marigny (sale of March–April 1782) and to Count de La Touche.

'Petit point' tapestry,
early 18th century
Wool. 3.500 x 0.830. Inv. 263

Manufacture des Gobelins
The Dessert, early 18th century
After Anne Vallayer-Coster
(1744–1818)
Wool. 0.580 x 0.660. Inv. 265

Manufacture des Gobelins
The Breakfast, early 18th century
After Anne Vallayer-Coster
(1744–1818)
Wool. 0.580 x 0.660. Inv. 265

The Manufacture de Beauvais reached its height between 1734 and 1753 thanks to the collaboration of Jean-Baptiste Oudry (1686–1755) and to its new director A. Besnier. Immediately after his appointment as the successor of the painter Duplessis in July 1726, Oudry, who was aware of the shift in tastes, encouraged the renewal of composition and of the conception of the models. We owe him *The Comedies of Molière*, then, in 1735, a series of refined verdures, and one year later *The Fables of La Fontaine*, whose success was such that they were subsequently picked up by Aubusson.

The six tapestries of the Grand Bureau [114] belong to this line of production. They originally were part of the decoration of the school of Soreze (Cantal) and the count bought them from the antique dealer Seligmann.

François Boucher (1703–1770) greatly contributed to the reputation of the Beauvais workshops. Already in 1736, he had painted fourteen compositions of the *Fêtes Italiennes*. The *Fisher Girl* [175], the fourth of this series, bears the marks of Besnier and Oudry on its blue border.

At the Salon of 1742, Boucher exhibited a series of sketches which are now in the Museum of Besançon, and which were to be used by Dumont for the *Chinese Tapestry*.

Manufacture des Gobelins
Supraporte, *c.* 1775–1785
Wool and silk. 1.030 x 1.960
Inv. 331

The Aubusson workshops borrowed the subjects of six pieces from Beauvais, simplifying and modifying them to some extent, and seeking inspiration mostly in the prints Huquier had done after works of Boucher. The four hangings, the *Chinese Dance*, the *Toilet of the Sultana* [330], the *Chinese Garden*, and the *Audience of the Chinese Emperor* [456] were made at Aubusson. They were part of the collection of Nissim de Camondo and the count kept them. Because these chinoiseries were an aspect of eighteenth-century art, they blend perfectly into the decoration of his town-house.

Seeking to mark his distances from the 'esprit bergerie', Casanova (1727–1802), the brother of the famous writer, treated his figures with realism, as can be seen in *Fishing with a Net* [264], but above all in the *Gypsies' Rest* [619].

Beauvais wove numerous seat covers, as well as valances and other decorative hangings. Those decorating the windows of the Salon Huet were done in 1785/86, as attested by the descriptions made on the occasion of their delivery in the book Badin devoted to the production of this manufacture. Thanks to this publication, we know that towards the end of the eighteenth century, De Menou, who was then administrator, asked various painters to design hangings; among them was Lavallée-Poussin who, in 1792, conceived four episodes in the life of Alexander.

The two supraportes [331] representing *Alexander Kneeling before the Tomb of Darius* and *The Queens of Persia at Alexander's Feet* were no doubt part of this sequence.

The four panels of *petit point* tapestry addorning the dining room [263] belonged to Count Nissim. Their flower vases framed in a border of fruit and foliage are very characteristic of this technique, as are the seat covers of the Nogaret furniture [462].

As all these examples show, the count took particular care to make

his house pleasant and welcoming, and it was with this in view that he also chose eighteenth-century silks for the curtains of the various rooms.

Manufacture d'Aubusson
The Toilet of the Sultana, c. 1750–1755
Wool and silk. 2.450 x 3.100. Inv. 330

Sculpture

Sculpture is without question a domain in which Moïse de Camondo did not assemble a set of works as significant as in other disciplines. With the exception of a few large sculptures of essentially decorative merit, one may nevertheless note a fine group of works in which portrait is the dominant genre.

Two famous bronzes, *Child with Bird* and *Child with Nest* [325], had been erroneously attributed to Pigalle, but Jean-René Gaborit has determined that these casts were made after two terracottas by

Jean-Jacques Caffieri (1725–1792)
Fidelity, c. 1769
White marble. Height: 0.480
Inv. 163

Pierre-Philippe Thomire
(1751–1843), after Jean-Antoine
Houdon (1741–1828)
Bust of a *Black Woman,*
early 18th century
Patinated bronze
0.750 x 0.480 x 0.300. Inv. 259

Jean-Antoine Houdon (1741–1828)
Summer, c. 1785
White marble. Height: 0.470
Inv. 165

Jean-Baptiste Nini (1717–1786)
Catherine II of Russia, 1771
Terracotta. Height: 0.155. Inv. 420

Charles-Antoine Bridan (1730–1805), now in the Chartres Museum, and inspired by antique marbles of the Borghese collection. Jean-Jacques Caffieri (1725–1792), one of the best portraitists of his day, was primarily famous for his busts, although he occasionally turned to allegories, such as his *Fidelity,* the signed and dated (1769) plaster of which is now in the Museum [784], together with a marble version [163].

Jean-Baptiste (Giovanni Battista) Nini was born in Urbino in 1717. As the son of an engraver, it was in this art that he first began to work before taking charge of a crystal-works near Madrid. Having moved to Paris about 1758, he remained there until 1772, at which date he moved to the Val-de-Loire, to the Château de Chaumont, where he was to die in 1786. His name remains associated with a highly specific product—moulded terracotta medallions, representing profile busts of a large number of prominent figures of his day. It appears that this activity had already begun when he was still living in Paris, but it was at Chaumont, and in collaboration with Jacques Le Ray, that it would reach its full development. This led to the creation of a striking gallery of portraits, of which the Museum now owns sixteen very fine specimens [414–429].

Terracotta was also the favourite material of Claude Michel, also known as Clodion (1738–1814). He created a very large number of small decorative sculptures, their subject matter presenting a rather anacreontic view of antiquity which is not devoid of sensuality. His two busts of bacchantes [411], now in the Petit Bureau, are outstanding for their liveliness and delicacy.

Jean-Antoine Houdon (1741–1828) dominated his age both in

monumental sculpture and in realistic portraiture. Four of his works were assembled by Moïse de Camondo. As a pendant to his well-known allegory of *Winter* from 1783, Houdon executed a marble statue of *Summer* in 1785. The two busts belonging to the Museum, one in marble [165], the other in plaster with a terracotta patina, were based on the latter [616]. Houdon was greatly inspired by children. His remarkable busts of his daughter Sabine or of the Brongniart children are rightly famous. Though less familiar than these two, the plaster bust of the little *Anne Audéoud* [695], daughter of a Genovese banker, is equally charming. The *Bust of a Black Woman* presented in the dining room was acquired

Claude Michel (Clodion)
(1738–1814)
Two busts of *Bacchantes*,
end 18th century
Terracotta. Height: 0.170. Inv. 411

in 1932 from Camoin [259]. About 1781, at the request of the Duke of Chartres, later known as Philippe-Egalité, Houdon executed a fountain representing a white marble bather, on whose shoulders a black woman, executed in lead, was pouring water. The piece was intended for the Folie de Monceau, (or 'de Chartres'), which has now become one of the most famous gardens in Paris. Except for the bather, now in the Metropolitan Museum in New York, the figures were lost during the Revolution; Houdon had however kept a plaster bust of the black woman, which he later used in an allegory celebrating the emancipation of the black slaves. The bronze bust in the Camondo collection bears an inscription according to which it was cast by Thomire after Houdon. Therefore, the presence of this work in the vicinity of the Parc Monceau, hardly appears fortuitous.

Jean-Antoine Houdon (1741–1828)
Presumed portrait of *Anne Audéoud*,
c. 1780
Plaster. Height: 0.500. Inv. 695

Painting

When Moïse de Camondo set himself the goal of reconstituting the ideal eighteenth-century residence, he was quite naturally led to become a collector of paintings. In the Age of Enlightenment, this art was still assured of a dominant position, even though its role was undergoing a profound transformation. To be sure, decorative painting, so intimately connected to architecture, maintained its prerogatives, but during the same period, easel painting became increasingly fashionable. The Camondo collection is a perfect reflection of this ambivalence.

The principles decreed by the Académie Royale, and made more stringent by Lebrun, were still compulsory. The various genres were still classified according to an immutable hierarchy. History painting remained the pre-eminently noble genre. Next came portrait painting, and finally, landscape, still-life, and genre painting which were considered less prestigious.

The Camondo collection of paintings illustrates a thoroughly personal choice and presents a twofold interest: first it permits one to study a body of works of the highest quality; and secondly it represents the particular sensibility of an art lover and his time.

It was in 1921 that Seligmann sold Moïse de Camondo a set of works that are among his most charming acquisitions: the eight sketches by Jean-Baptiste Oudry (1686–1755) representing the hunts of Louis XV [440]. It has been established that this series was related to the elaboration of one of the handsome hangings woven at the Gobelins in the eighteenth century. The original commission, made in 1733, concerned at least three compositions, a figure which increased to nine a few years later, as attested by the dates beside the signatures on most of the sketches. The ninth of these, the *Stag at Bay among the Franchard Rocks*, is now in a private collection. Those of the Camondo collection had belonged to Jules-Robert de Cotte (1683–1767), director of the Gobelins and son of the famous architect. Eight of the definitive cartoons were integrated into the decoration of the Appartements des Chasses in Fontainebleau during the nineteenth century; the ninth is in the Louvre. Two complete sets were woven on high-warp looms on the basis of these compositions; one of them, executed in the Monmerqué workshops, was intended to hang in the king's apartments in Compiègne, and is still on view in that palace today. Another one, produced by Audran's workshop, was acquired in 1749 by the Infante Don Philip, Duke of Parma, son-in-law of Louis XV, and is now to be seen in the Pitti Palace in Florence.

Since medieval times, weavers had made abundant use of hunting themes. In the sixteenth century, the Brussels series of the *Hunts*

The Salon Huet
The room is called after the famous series of paintings by Jean-Baptiste Huet depicting an arcadian romance.

105

Jean-Baptiste Oudry (1686–1755)
The Meet at the Puys du Roi at Compiègne, 1733
Sketch for a tapestry cartoon (*The Hunts of Louis XV*, Manufacture des Gobelins)
Oil on canvas. 0.450 x 0.820
Inv. 440

of Maximilian represented the acme of the genre. The scenes painted by Oudry are a manifest return to this tradition and also make reference to the *History of the King* series woven under the reign of Louis XIV. As we know, hunting was a daily pastime when the kings were in Compiègne and Fontainebleau, and was marked by an unparalleled display of luxury. Oudry strove to render the various episodes of the hunt as accurately as possible, representing the precise locations where they occurred.

The *Meet at the Puys du Roi at Compiègne* represents the moment when the Count of Toulouse, Master of the Royal Hunt, reports to the king on the preparations for the hunt. Behind them, the main crossroads of the forest offers a threefold perspective, enlivened by a great gathering of riders and hounds.

Several highly characteristic sites of the same forest are evoked in five other compositions: *The Death of the Stag at Saint-Jean-aux-Bois, The Stag Hunt near Royallieu, The King holding the Blood-Hound at the Crossroads of the Puits-Solitaire, The Old Pack uncoupled at la Petite Patte-d'Oie,* and *The Hounds at the Crossroads of L'Embrassade.* The site of *The Kill,* which depicts the moment in which the offals are thrown to the hounds, has not been identified.

It is worth remembering that Moïse de Camondo, who was very fond of hunting, indulged in his passion regularly, with a group of

Jean-Baptiste Oudry (1686–1755)
The Kill, 1745
Sketch for a tapestry cartoon (*The Hunts of Louis XV,* Manufacture des Gobelins)
Oil on canvas. 0.440 x 0.340
Inv. 440

friends, in his property at Aumont near Senlis. The fact that he had Oudry's sketches in his collection, is far from being fortuitous, and is rather a reflection of his marked fondness for this sort of pastime. This also accounts for his purchase of other paintings representing hunting scenes, by Carle Vernet (1758–1836) [571], Sweebach (1769–1823) [789, 790] and Alfred de Dreux (1810–1860) [787].

Undoubtedly as a result of the count's personal tastes, there are only two mythological paintings in the Museum's collection: the *Danaë* [704], attributed to Louis-Jean-François Lagrenée (1725–1805), and the *Bacchante* [113], by Louise-Elisabeth Vigée-Lebrun

Louise-Elisabeth Vigée Lebrun
(1755–1842)
Bacchante, 1785
Oil on panel. 1.090 x 0.880. Inv. 113

Louise-Elisabeth Vigée Lebrun
Geneviève-Sophie le Coulteux du Molay,
1788
Oil on canvas. 1.000 x 0.790. Inv. 172

(1755–1842). This last painting—another version, on canvas, is in a private collection—was acquired from Seligmann in 1923. In view of its genre, the work is exceptional in this artist's *œuvre*. Produced on commission for Count de Vaudreuil, it was exhibited at the Salon of 1785, where David's *Oath of the Horatii* was also shown for the first time.

Madame Vigée-Lebrun was best known as a portraitist, at the service of the queen and of the aristocracy. The portrait of *Geneviève-Sophie le Coulteux du Molay* [172] was painted in 1788. In the course of the summer, the artist stayed at Malmaison, which was then the property of this family; 'Madame du Molay', Vigée-

108

François-Hubert Drouais
(1727–1775)
*Armand-Léon de Serrent in the Uniform
of a Drummer of the Royal-Cavalerie,*
1769
Oil on canvas. 0.690 x 0.550. Inv. 168

Lebrun noted in her memoirs, 'was a pretty and very fashionable young woman. Her wit was not electrifying, but she understood that of other people with intelligence.' The naturalness in her pose and expression, along with the elegance of her dress, admirably express both the painter's sensibility and her friendly complicity with her model.

Adélaïde Labille-Guiard (1749–1803) was regarded as a rival of Madame Vigée-Lebrun who undeniably outshone her. Yet Labille-Guiard's qualities were in no way inferior to those of Vigée-Lebrun, particularly in the execution of male portraits, among which the one of *Prince Charles-Roger de Bauffremont* is a case in point. The definitive version, now at Versailles, was shown at the 1791 Salon. The sketch, bought by Count Moïse in 1923 from Wildenstein, was done in 1789 and shows a craftsmanship that is both energetic, and penetratingly observant.

The same qualities are found in Joseph-Siffred Duplessis' (1725–1802) portrait of *Jacques Necker* [435], Director General of Finances in 1777. Duplessis' taste for accuracy, discretion and subtlety, and his avoidance of flattery, make this artist, who was the official painter of Louis XVI, one of the best portraitists of his generation.

In 1920 Seligmann sold Moïse de Camondo two attractive portraits by François-Hubert Drouais (1727–1775). One of the two young boys, the sons of the Marquess de Serrent, can be seen wearing the uniform of the Prince de Condé, the other that of a drummer of the Royal-Cavalerie [168]. Both of them perfectly reflect the artist's somewhat mannered treatment of the world of childhood.

The miniature by Jean-Baptiste Isabey (1767–1855), representing the four children of Joachim Murat and Caroline Bonaparte [231]—Achille, Letizia, Lucien, and Louise, born in 1801, 1802, 1803, and 1805 respectively—is more persuasive and tender. This work originally belonged to the collection of Count Nissim, Moïse's father.

The series of nineteenth-century portraits assembled by Moïse were to be admirably supplemented by the acquisition at an auction on 16 November 1932, of a striking family portrait [567] signed Jean-Baptiste-André Gautier-Dagoty (1740–1786), which had already been sold at auction on 17 December 1920. The identity of this family has not yet been established. The gathering is apparently being held in a hall of monumental proportions, possibly a library, which is partly concealed by a drapery. The busts of Henri IV and of Louis XV can be made out in the background, an obvious homage to the Bourbons. A large oval uncompleted painting appears to honour a departed relative, whose bust, in a cuirass, is shown being crowned by the personification of Time. One of the female figures holds a palette and a brush, the other a pencil. Three of the men wear the cross of the knights of the Royal Order of Saint-Louis which rewards Catholic officers having spent at least ten years in the royal army. To judge from the style of the clothing, the painting may date from the 1770s. The wealth of the setting and the clothes suggest that the people assembled here are of a relatively high social level.

Although landscape, in the eighteenth century, did not enjoy a prestige comparable to that of history or portrait painting, it was

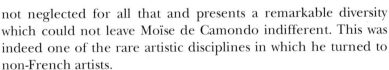

Joseph-Siffred Duplessis (1725–1802)
Jacques Necker, c. 1770
Oil on canvas. Inv. 435

Adélaïde Labille-Guiard (1749–1803)
Prince Charles-Roger de Bauffremont,
c. 1790
Oil on canvas. 0.340 x 0.230. Inv. 169

not neglected for all that and presents a remarkable diversity which could not leave Moïse de Camondo indifferent. This was indeed one of the rare artistic disciplines in which he turned to non-French artists.

Eighteenth-century painters of Venice developed a style of urban landscape that was quite typical of Venetian aesthetics—the *veduta*. After Canaletto, the great specialist was Francesco Guardi (1712–1792). His countless views of the city—a complete renovation of the genre—charm the beholder with the liveliness of the brushwork and their almost impressionistic luminosity. Perfect instances of this are Guardi's *View of the Piazzetta with the Doges' Palace and the Riva degli Schiavoni*, together with its pendant representing *San Giorgio Maggiore, the Dogana and La Salute* [437]. Both had belonged to the collection of Baron Albert de Rothschild, and were sold to the count by André Weil in 1932. Antonio Morassi has rightly stressed the importance of these works, painted about 1780, which are among the most perfect of the

Jean-Baptiste Isabey (1767–1855)
The Children of Murat, King of Naples,
c. 1810
Oil on marble. 0.240 x 0.180. Inv. 231

Jean-Baptiste-André Gautier-Dagoty
(1740–1786)
Family Portrait, c. 1770
Oil on canvas. 1.300 x 1.940. Inv. 567

painter's mature period. The view of the *Piazza San Marco* with the Campanile and the Church of San Gemignano and that of *La Piazzetta* towards San Giorgio Maggiore [436] had been in the collections of Sir Richard Wallace, Sir John Murray-Scott, and Lady Sackville-West. According to Morassi, the architecture was painted by Francesco Guardi's son Giacomo (1764–1835). The collaboration between the two painters consequently situates these two works after 1780. Two architectural *capriccios* [702] afford a charming instance of a genre in which Guardi gives a freer hand to his penchant for reverie and unreality.

A single painter, Hubert Robert (1733–1808), dominated French landscape painting all through the second half of the eighteenth century. Profoundly influenced by a long stay in Italy, he brought back a vast trove of recollections to which the artist was to turn

Francesco Guardi (1712–1793)
The Piazzetta, mid-18th century
Oil on canvas. 0.260 x 0.350. Inv. 436

Francesco Guardi
Piazza San Marco, mid-18th century
Oil on canvas. 0.260 x 0.350. Inv. 436

114

Francesco Guardi (1712–1793)
*View of the Piazzetta with the Doges'
Palace and the Riva degli Schiavoni,*
second half 18th century
Oil on canvas. 0.680 x 1.010. Inv. 437

Francesco Guardi (1712–1793)
*San Giorgio Maggiore, the Dogana and
La Salute,* second half 18th century
Oil on canvas. 0.680 x 1.010. Inv. 437

throughout his life, particularly when working as a decorator. The two very fine mountain landscapes in the vestibule [34] show how faithful Robert had remained to the classical tradition. Their format suggests they were intended to be integrated into the decoration of an unidentified dwelling.

Ruins were among his favourite subjects. He quite spontaneously embraced the sensibility of his age on this point, as can be seen in a little composition with monuments of antiquity [443]. Gardens, both real and imaginary, constantly inspired him. Indeed, he himself was an occasional creator of English-style gardens at Versailles or Méréville. The two landscapes in the library illustrate

Francesco Guardi (1712–1793)
Venetian capriccio, 1770
Oil on canvas. 0.200 x 0.115. Inv. 702

this aspect of his work. One, representing the *Water Jet* [618], is evocative of the gardens of Italy and the Roman villas; the other [617] shows a rustic pavilion very much like the *fabriques* of which so many were to be seen in the parks of Ile-de-France, and which also appear in a *View of Ermenonville,* with the tomb of Jean-Jacques Rousseau [708].

Hubert Robert was also a keen observer of a more day-to-day and concrete reality: the streets and monuments of Paris, as in the

Hubert Robert (1733–1808)
Mountain Landscape,
end 18th century
Oil on canvas
2.820 x 1.300. Inv. 34

Hubert Robert
Rustic Pavilion in a Park,
end 18th century
Oil on canvas
0.720 x 0.550. Inv. 617

French School, end 18th century
*View of the Lawn and Stables of
Chantilly on the Day of the Feast in
1785*, 1785
Watercolour. 0.345 x 0.590. Inv. 719

Nicolas and Jean-Baptiste Raguenet
(French School, 18th century)
The Samaritaine and the Pont Neuf,
1755
Oil on canvas. 0.460 x 0.850. Inv. 570

Victor-Jean Nicolle (1757–1826)
Porte Saint-Denis, end 18th century
Watercolour. 0.095 x 0.140. Inv. 716

views of the Porte Saint-Denis and the Porte Saint-Martin [442]. Hubert Robert was not the only painter who demonstrated a lively interest in Parisian life. Several of his contemporaries also worked in the same vein. Nicolas and Jean-Baptiste Raguenet, father and son, turned out a whole series of views of Paris, characterized mainly by a scrupulous accuracy and a careful realism. Today they constitute priceless documents of the Parisian past. In the Salon Bleu can be seen the views of the Pont Neuf, the Pont Marie [569], and the Samaritaine [570]. Finally, in this same genre, there is a small watercolour by Victor-Jean Nicolle (1754–1826), showing the 'grand boulevards' and the Porte Saint-Denis [716].

Pierre-Antoine Demachy
(1723–1807)
Architectural Capriccio with the Luxembourg Palace, 1774
Oil on canvas. 0.650 x 0.800. Inv. 565

While often inspired by the monuments of Paris, the works of Pierre-Antoine Demachy (1723–1807) reveal a different outlook. It seems that he never left France, but he was thoroughly influenced by the world of Piranesi: he had the same penchant, both meditative and visionary, for theatrical perspectives and colossal architecture, sometimes in ruins. This accounts for the way in which the architectural fantasies showing the Luxembourg Palace [565] and the Louvre Colonnade [566], mingle dream and reality in an unexpected way.

In the opinion of Moïse de Camondo and his contemporaries, nothing could better express the charm of the eighteenth century than genre painting. Thus the privileged position the count granted it in his collection comes as no surprise, see, for instance, the large compositions [186] after which the Salon Huet was named, and who are entirely representative of the great decorative cycles so widely appreciated at that time. For all his ambition, Jean-Baptiste Huet (1745–1811) had not managed to make himself a name as a history painter, but was none the less admitted to the Académie as an animal painter. His talent was no less brilliant for all that, witness his obvious gift as a decorator. In 1900 Camondo purchased from Seligmann the seven panels and two supraportes. According to a document in the Museum's ar-

French School, 18th century
*Composition with Palm Tree, Parasol,
and Cats,* mid-18th century
Oil on canvas. 0.490 x 0.190. Inv. 174

Jean-Baptiste Huet (1745–1811)
The Shepherdess in Love, second half
18th century
Oil on canvas. 2.170 x 1.450. Inv. 186

chives, the lot came from the Château of Benguet, near Mont-de-Marsan, which belonged to Baroness de Lonjon. The third supra-porte, dated 1776, was only acquired in 1927. Nothing proves that it was part of the original series, and we know neither when, nor for whom, nor indeed in what circumstances it was created.

The six main canvases seem to relate the loves of a shepherd and a shepherdess, whose messengers, until their tender and happy reunion, are in turn a dove and a dog. One may be tempted to compare the work of Huet and the very famous compositions painted at Louveciennes by Fragonard, about 1771, for Madame du Barry. In both cases the theme of the progress of love serves

Jean-Baptiste Hilaire
(1753–after 1822)
Reading in a Park, second half
18th century
Oil on canvas. 0.170 x 0.220. Inv. 438

as a pretext for the creation of large mural compositions. However, Huet's more meticulous and laborious technique, still marked by Boucher's influence, does not compare with the dazzling bravado of Fragonard's brush. Not until 1915 did Frick acquire some of the latter's paintings, so that the acquisition of the works of Huet, fifteen years earlier, undeniably make Camondo a precursor.

The great number of small genre paintings, which cannot all be mentioned, reflect both the choice of an informed amateur and that of a nostalgic lover of the eighteenth century. *Bad Tidings* [706] painted by Jean-Baptiste-Marie Pierre (1713–1789) in 1740, is fascinating because of its froth of gold and pink silks, and the sense of disarray it conveys. Jean-Baptiste Hilaire (1753–after 1822), on the other hand, in his *Reading in a Park* [438], expresses both inner peace and serenity.

Nineteenth-century art was not neglected by Moïse de Camondo who proved himself capable of selecting several significant works. This is the case of the curious painting by Henri Philippoteaux (1815–1884), representing the *Gentlemen of the Duke of Orléans: the 'Habit de Saint-Cloud'* [568], acquired at the Duc de Vendôme sale in 1931. There are several versions of this ironical view of society under the Ancien Régime. Quite a number of early nineteenth-century paintings have been assembled in Nissim's room, hunting and horses being the dominant themes. Special mention should

Jean-Baptiste-Marie Pierre
(1713–1789)
Bad Tidings, 1740
Oil on paper mounted on canvas
0.235 x 0.185. Inv. 706

Jacques François-Joseph Swebach
(Fontaine) (1769–1823)
Mailcoach and Relay,
early 19th century
Oil on canvas. 0.720 x 0.580. Inv. 789

Horace Vernet (1789–1863)
The Calèche, 1836
Oil on canvas. 0.600 x 1.000. Inv. 791

be made of *The Calèche* [791], by Horace Vernet (1789–1863), signed and dated 1836.

In the Salon Bleu, formerly Béatrice de Camondo's bedroom, the visitor may be surprised to discover eight watercolour landscapes and seascapes by Jongkind (1819–1891). This collection, assembled by Isaac de Camondo, whose ties with several representatives of the Impressionist movement is well known, was bequeathed by the latter to his cousin Moïse.

The subtle nuances which have affected the disposition of various items about the house are not without significance. While the eighteenth century reigns supreme on the main floor which

was exclusively used for receptions, the upper floor, primarily that of private rooms, is characterized by a greater freedom and expresses, through the more individual tastes of members of the family, the touching reality of everyday life.

Johan Bartold Jongkind (1819–1891)
La Côte Saint-André, 2 April 1884
Watercolour. 0.310 x 0.450. Inv. 574

Index

Bibliography

Catalogue
Jean Messelet, *Musée Nissim de Camondo*, Paris 1936
(numerous re-editions)

Furniture
François de Salverte, *Les Ebénistes du XVIIIᵉ siècle*,
Paris 1927
Pierre Verlet, Le Mobilier Royal Français I, Paris
1945; II, Paris 1955; IV, Paris 1990
Geoffrey de Bellaigue, *The James A. de Rothschild
Collection at Waddesdon Manor, Furniture Clocks and
Gilt Bronzes*, II, Freiburg 1974
Patricia Lemonnier, *Weisweiler*, Maurice Segoura
(ed.), Paris 1983
La Folie d'Artois, Paris 1988
Alexandre Pradère, *Les Ebénistes Français de Louis
XIV à la Révolution*, Paris 1989

Gilt Bronze Furniture
Svend Eriksen, *Early Neo-Classicism in France*,
London 1974
Pierre Verlet, *Les bronzes dorés du XVIIIᵉ siècle*,
Paris 1987
Christian Baulez, Notes sur quelques meubles et
objets d'art des appartements intérieurs de Louis
XVI et Marie-Antoinette, *Revue du Louvre* 1978,
5/6, pp. 359–373
Christian Baulez, *Hôtel de Roquelaure, Le Faubourg
Saint-Germain, la rue Saint-Dominique* (exh. cat.),
Paris, Musée Rodin, 1984, pp. 164–176

Silverware
Gérard Mabille, Orfèvrerie Française des XVIᵉ,
XVIIᵉ, XVIIIᵉ siècles, *Catalogue raisonné des
collections du Musée des Arts Décoratifs et du Musée
Nissim de Camondo*, Paris 1984

Porcelain
Marcelle Brunet and Tamara Préaud, *Sèvres des
origines à nos jours*, Freiburg, 1978
Aileen Dawson, The Eden Service, *Apollo*, April
1980, pp. 288–297
Michael Hall, The Chartres Forth Service, *Apollo*,
June 1986, pp. 386–389

Carpets and Tapestries
Jules Guiffrey, *Inventaire général du mobilier de la
Couronne sous Louis XIV*, 2 vols., Paris 1885
Maurice Fenaille, *Etat des tapisseries de la
Manufacture des Gobelins depuis son origine jusqu'à
nos jours*, 6 vols., Paris 1903–1923
Jules Badin, *La Manufacture des tapisseries de
Beauvais*, Paris 1909
Pierre Verlet, Les Paravents de Savonnerie
pendant la première moitié du XVIIIᵉ siècle,
L'Information d'Histoire de l'Art, May–June 1967,
pp. 106–118
Pierre Verlet, *The James A. de Rothschild collection at
Waddesdon Manor, The Savonnerie*, Freiburg 1982

Sculpture
Louis Réau, *Houdon, sa vie et son œuvre*, 2 vols.,
Paris 1964

Painting
Jean-Baptiste Oudry (exh. cat.), Paris, Grand Palais,
1982–1983
Marguerite Jallut, Le Portrait du Prince de
Bauffremont par Madame Labille-Guiard, *Revue
du Louvre* 1962, 5, pp. 217–222
Anne-Marie Passez, *Adélaïde Labille-Guiard*,
Paris 1973
Antonio Morassi, *Guardi, Antonio
et Francesco Guardi*, 2 vols., Venice 1973
Mariane Roland-Michel, *Anne Vallayer-Coster*,
Paris 1970

Contents

Musées et Monuments de France
Published with the support of the Fondation Paribas

Books in print

PARIS   The Carnavalet Museum

PARIS   The Gustave Moreau Museum

VERSAILLES   The Palace

BAYONNE   The Bonnat Museum

ECOUEN   The Château

LYONS   The Museum of Fine Arts

GRENOBLE   The Museum of Art

ROUEN   The Museum of Fine Arts

ANTIBES   The Picasso Museum

PARIS   The National Museum of Modern Art
    Paintings & Sculptures

NANCY   The Museum of Fine Arts

PARIS   The National Museum of Modern Art
    Cabinet d'Art graphique

LYONS   The Textile Museum

NANTES   The Museum of Fine Arts

SAINT-ETIENNE   The Museum of Modern Art

PARIS   The Nissim de Camondo Museum

COLMAR   The Unterlinden Museum

LIMOGES   The National Museum Adrien Dubouché

BORDEAUX   The Museum of Aquitaine

PARIS   Bibliothèque Nationale

DIJON   The Museum of Fine Arts

QUIMPER   The Museum of Fine Arts

SAINT-TROPEZ   The Annonciade Museum

LISBOA   The National Coach Museum

CAEN   The Museum of Fine Arts

BESANÇON   The Museum of Fine Arts and
    Archeology

MULHOUSE   The National Automobile Museum
    (Schlumpf Collection)

Photography by Hugo Maertens, Bruges
Edited by Artescriptum, Ghent
Designed by Stéphan Alberty, Brussels
Production by Ludion, Brussels

Typeset in Baskerville by Artescriptum, Ghent
Lithography by Beta Graphics, Lede
Printed by Erasmus, Wetteren
Bound by Splichal, Turnhout

© 1991 Musées et Monuments de France
Didier Marty
41, Avenue de l'Opéra
75002 Paris
Tel.: 42 98 01 36
ISBN (pbk.) 2-297333-14-3
ISBN (hbk.) 2-297333-15-1
Dépôt légal: September 1991
Reprinted in 1995